Dream-Biz.com

Design Your Future and Live Your Dreams in the e-Economy!

Burke Hedges

PUBLISHING **&** RESOURCE BOOKS

Books To Build A Better You!

Dream-Biz.com

*Design Your Future
and Live Your Dreams
in the e-Economy!*

by Burke Hedges

Printed in the United States of America
First edition June 1999

ISBN: 1-891279-02-5
Published by INTI Publishing
Tampa, FL

The phrase "Interactive Distribution™" is used with permission from Internet Services Corporation.

Cover design and layout by Laurie Winters

dedication

One night at the dinner table I asked my eight-year-old son, Nathen, what he wishes to be when he grows up.

"An entrepreneur, Daddy," he replied.

"What does that mean to you?" I asked.

"Lots of money. No school. No bosses. And I can go to as many NBA basketball games as I want," he replied.

He was describing freedom! Smart kid.

I dedicate this book to my four children, Burke, Nathen, Spencer, and Aspen Marie, and to the many people around the world who are seeking more freedom for themselves and their families through free enterprise.

May they find the golden key to their dreams in the e-economy.

Also By Burke Hedges

- *Who Stole the American Dream?*

- *You Can't Steal Second with Your Foot on First!*

- *You, Inc.*

- *Copycat Marketing 101*

- *Read & Grow Rich*

acknowledgment

Normally I would use this opportunity to recognize individuals who played a key role in bringing one of my books to life.

But this time I'd like to acknowledge not separate individuals, but an entire team. Thank you, Team INTI Publishing, for your unselfish effort and unwavering commitment to our common goal of creating a quality, much-needed message in record time.

I salute all of you for the countless hours you gave to the research, design, rewrites, and final editing of this book. From the bottom of my heart I say, "Thank you, Team INTI. You truly are THE BEST!"

I love you all,

contents

"This Is the Greatest Tool Ever Invented!"

We used tools in the past to leverage our muscles.
We use tools today to leverage our minds.
–Bill Gates, Microsoft Founder & CEO

I wish you could have seen the expression on my mother's face when I took her on her first tour of the Internet.

"This is the greatest tool ever invented!" she exclaimed with delight as we zapped from website to website with a point and a click.

Introduction

I must say I was more than surprised at my mother's reaction. Fact is, I was shocked! You see, my mother is the least technical person I know. She's a people person, and she's a real go-getter — she's raised millions of dollars for I-don't-know-how-many charities over the years. If you want something done, all you have to do is ask my mom. It WILL get done!

But my mother is clueless when it comes to anything technical! CLUELESS! She can set the electric alarm clock and the temperature in the oven, but that's about it. But despite her technical limitations, she took to the Internet like a duck to water! Once she got over her initial fears ("I don't have to learn to... how do you say, *program* this thing, do I?") she was off and running.

Tools Are Only as Good as the People Operating Them!

My mother was thrilled to learn that the whole world was only a point and click away. And it only took her a few minutes to recognize the Net's immediate value and long-term potential.

She loved her new tool! Loved the convenience. Loved the ease of use. Loved the fact she could buy (and sell) virtually anything online that she could buy at a store. She could shop from home... research any topic... buy airline tickets and reserve hotel rooms... visit museums all over the world... e-mail her six grandchildren... play games... chat with friends... and download recipes.

Last time I talked to Mom, she and Dad were going shopping for a computer.

I tell you this story about my mom for two reasons. First, to let you know just how easy it is to hook up a computer and "surf the Internet" these days. That hasn't always been the case. Just a few short years ago you had to learn a long list of keyboard commands to run a simple software program. It was like learning a new language. Not so anymore. The Internet is user-friendly and getting friendlier by the day! *If my mom can surf the Internet within minutes, anybody can!*

Second, I want you to understand that the computer wired to the Internet is a tool. An awesome, powerful tool — but a tool, nonetheless. It may well be, as my mom says, "the greatest tool ever invented" — *but it's still just a tool.* Like a shovel. Or a can opener. Or a car. Tools were invented as a way for people to save time and effort. But in the end, tools are only as good as the people operating them.

The Internet as a Business Tool

The Internet is a great tool to enhance our personal lives, but it's also a great business tool. When you think about it, the Internet is all of today's best business tools rolled into one — and then some! It's a typewriter... a fax... a phone... a VCR... a TV... a dictating machine... a catalog... a letter... an answering machine... a virtual mall... a virtual office... all linked up to a network of millions of computers in homes, schools, and offices all over the world. Wow!

This tool is so powerful that a single person can build a multi-million-dollar business from the keyboard of one Internet-linked computer! But a different person can take that same computer with the same Internet access and sit it on a desk and never turn it on! How much profit will this computer generate? Zero.

Same tool.

Same business potential.

Different results.

The point is that people run tools, tools don't run people. Right now thousands of people are positioning themselves to use the Internet as a tool to profit from Internet commerce — e-commerce, as it's being called. Some of these people don't even own a computer yet. Others own the most jazzed-up personal computer money can buy. But their success won't be determined by the size and type of their computer — their tool. Their success will be determined by the person operating the tool.

High Tech, High Touch

Every business is a people business. Whether you're offering products, such as shoes or shower caps... or whether you're offering services, such as long distance phone service or long-term loans — *you are still in the people business!*

Whether you're an independent business owner of an "old economy" business with a bricks-and-mortar address... or the owner of a new "e-economy" business with an Internet address, *you're still in the people business.*

No matter what business you're in, your success depends on your ability to communicate with people... listen to people... attract people... help people... sell to people... teach and train people... inspire people... share with people... and love people.

Without people on each end, a phone is nothing more than a big paperweight. Same with a computer. The Internet is a powerful tool, all right. Maybe the greatest tool ever invented. But we must never lose sight of the fact that it's still a tool to enrich the lives of other people.

Income Gap Becomes the Dream Gap

You've probably read that the income gap is widening — the rich keep getting richer investing in a raging bull stock market, and the super-smart "techies are raking in zillions making computers, developing software, and starting high-flying Internet companies.

While the sun has been shining on the fortunate few, most people are left standing in the rain! Average people, the vast majority of people who make up the middle class — still aren't getting ahead. They're just treading water, or worse, sinking deeper in debt.

As a result, there's another gap that's getting wider and wider by the day — the dream gap! The dream gap is the gap between what people dream for themselves and their families, and what they can *really afford.*

You see, dreams aren't just the property of the upper class. Average people have dreams, too. *People dream of financial independence.* But the reality is that most people are having to work longer hours, only to earn less money. *People dream of job security for themselves and their families.* But the reality is that massive layoffs continue. *People dream of a comfortable retirement and a college education for their kids.* But the reality is that savings levels are at an all-time low. *People dream of spending more time at home and taking family vacations every year.* But the reality is that Mom is working and Dad has a second job, so there's never enough time for the family.

What's the Solution?

This book will offer you the *solution to closing the dream gap. Dream-Biz.Com* will explain how average people can take advantage of the greatest economic boom in the history of the world.

E-commerce is getting ready to explode as we enter the New Millennium, and you can position yourself to profit from that boom in a big way — just as the super-rich and the super-smart people are doing.

This once-in-a-lifetime opportunity won't be around for long, so catch the wave while you can — and ride it to the top!

Design your future and live your dreams in the e-economy!

Part One

Dreaming Big Dreams

... 1 ...

The Internet: Where Dot.com Dreams Come True!

The Internet will shrink the world —
changing the fortunes of people,
companies, and countries.

–John Chambers, Cisco Systems CEO

The Internet is made for dreamers — "dot.com dreamers," I call them.

Jeff Bezos was one of the first dot.com dreamers in the short history of the Internet — and one of the most successful. He jumped on the Internet bandwagon in 1994, two years after President George

Bush signed legislation allowing the public to conduct commerce on the Net.

By 1997 — only three years after he started his Internet company — Jeff Bezos was a billionaire!

Here's his incredible story:

An e-Commerce Dreamer

Jeff Bezos wasn't just smart — he was a brain! He graduated from Princeton *summa cum laude* with a double major in electrical engineering and computer science. Two years after graduation, he took a job on Wall Street with Bankers Trust Company developing computer systems that helped manage $250 billion in assets. Two years after that, 26-year-old Bezos became the youngest vice president in the company's history. By 30, he was a multi-millionaire.

It looked like Bezos was on the fast track to become a Wall Street CEO. But he had a dream to own his own business... to be his own boss... and to call his own shots. He understood he'd never be able to do that working for someone else, no matter what job title was on his nameplate.

Bezos kept his eye out for business opportunities. Then one day in early 1994, he read a statistic that would change his life: *The Internet was growing at a rate of 2,300% a year!*

"Outside of a Petri dish, I'd never seen anything grow as fast as the Internet," he said. Bezos didn't know what business he would go into. He just knew it would be online. And he knew it would be soon.

Bezos made a list of 20 different products that could be sold online and ranked them according to which product would be easiest to sell. Books came in first. He resigned from his job and drew up a business plan for an Internet company on his laptop computer while his wife drove from New York to the West Coast.

He decided to call his new online venture

Amazon.com. As I write this, *Amazon.com* is a five-year-old company with a market capitalization of $25 billion, and the company has quickly become one of the most recognized brand names in North America.

e-Commerce Explosion

Bezos' daring enterprise was the first big success for e-commerce, and it focused the world's attention on the Internet's enormous commercial potential. Even though the jury is out as to when, if ever, Amazon.com will turn a profit, the company paved the way for an e-commerce explosion that is revolutionizing the way wealth is created.

To better understand the wealth-creating capacity of e-commerce, let's compare it to some other giant industries that have dominated the world economy — automobiles, retailing, and computer software.

Prior to the Internet, it took decades for a business owner to amass a billion dollars.

It took Henry Ford 23 years to reach his first billion.

Sam Walton needed 20 years to earn his first billion.

It even took Bill Gates 12 years to earn a billion.

It took Jeff Bezos three years to earn a billion on the Internet! According to *Fortune* magazine, Bezos was worth almost $9 billion in 1999, only five years after starting Amazon.com!

Internet fortunes are made in months or years — instead of decades. And the scary thing is, the Net is just in its infancy! The Net has been doubling every year for the past 11 years, according to Vint Cerf, president of the Internet Society. He predicts that by the end of 2000, there will be 300 million people online. *Wow!*

As Al Jolson used to say, *"Folks, you ain't seen nothin' yet!"*

Scores of reputable institutions are forecasting

incredible growth of the Internet and e-commerce in the next few years. Although the growth figures may vary widely, all forecasters agree that e-commerce will explode as it enters the 21st century.

Below are graphs charting the near-term growth of e-commerce and the number of Internet buyers based on forecasts by the International Data Corporation.

INTERNET COMMERCE

Graph 1:
Gross Revenues from e-Commerce

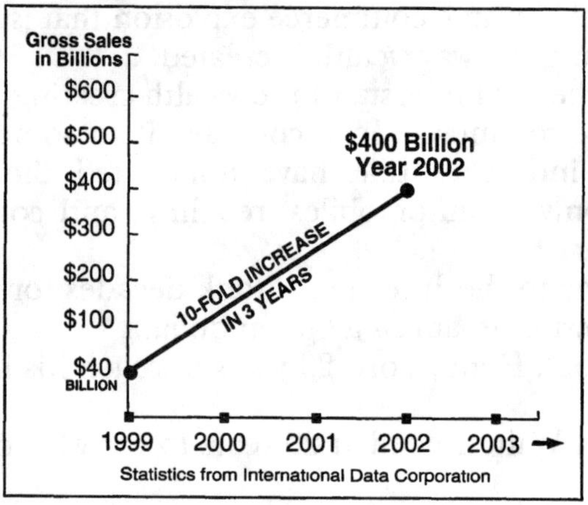

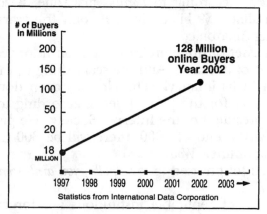

Graph 2:
Number of Buyers on the Internet

You only need to glance at these graphs to recognize that *the growth projections for e-commerce are mind-boggling!* A few short years from now, *e-commerce revenues are projected to increase 10-fold!...* and the number of *online buyers will exceed 100 million!* The world has never seen growth like this before! It's unbelievable! The e-commerce explosion isn't just a trend — it's a world-wide mega-shift in the buying/selling cycle!

Projections like these mean that a whole lot of people are going to make a whole lot of money during the coming decade. Folks, we're standing at the edge of an e-commerce explosion just as it's beginning to erupt, and those of us who are alert enough to position ourselves to take advantage of this incredible opportunity will stake a claim to hundreds of billions of dollars in the next few years.

Jeff Bezos saw this massive mega-trend unfolding in 1994, and he didn't hesitate. He understood the importance of being in the right place at the right time — and he jumped in with both feet. Three years later he was a multi-billionaire... and the big growth wave hasn't even started rolling in yet! Amazing!

I'm Happy for Jeff Bezos... But What About Me?

Jeff Bezos is living testimony to the power of dot.com dreaming, and his amazing success with e-commerce offers valuable lessons about the future of the Internet — the most amazing wealth-creating vehicle in the history of the world!

Hey, I'm happy for Bezos and all the other computer geniuses who are cashing in big on the Internet boom. More power to them.

But what about the rest of us mortals? What about average people like you and me? Is there a way we can profit from the Internet boom?

Up until very recently, the answer was "no." Only

the people with the brains to develop a popular Web browser, like the founders of Yahoo! or Netscape... or the people with big bucks to invest in fast-growing online companies, like Bill Gates... were making money on the Internet.

As for the rest of us — well, let's face facts: Most of us can't even program our VCRs, much less create an online bookstore from scratch. And as far as investing money in Internet stocks... well, most people are lucky to have some change left in their pockets after paying the monthly bills.

As a comic once observed, "There's just too much month at the end of the money" for most people. People who are lucky enough to get their hands on an extra grand or two would be wiser to pay down their credit card debt than to invest in an unproven Internet company.

That means that most of us are *paying* — instead of *being paid* to use the Net. Like always, most people are stuck building someone else's dream, rather than their own.

Are the masses destined to be left on the cyber sidewalk looking in, like all the other economic booms in years past?

Or is the Internet phenomenon different? Is there a way the "little" guys can make big profits on the Net?

Your Own Dream-Biz.com

Well, I'm delighted to announce that there is a way for average people to profit in a big way from the e-commerce explosion.

There is a way for the average person to start his or her own e-commerce business that could distribute thousands of dollars... perhaps even millions of dollars... worth of products and services a year.

It's a dream business that taps into the awesome power of the Internet. Which means that, like other successful Internet enterprises, it can be *built fast...* and it can be *built vast!*

It's an amazing concept I call "Dream-Biz.com."

Not only is the Dream-Biz.com concept available to average people, but it also has major advantages over every other Internet business out there. In fact, your Dream-Biz.com is as revolutionary as the Internet itself!

Okay, let's get started by talking about the first word in your online "dream-biz."

It's the word that can empower you to join the ranks of the dot.com dreamers.

That word is *dream...* and we'll start by talking about yours!

...2...

If You Want Big Results, You Gotta Dream Big Dreams!

All achievement and all earthly riches have their beginnings in an idea or a dream.

−Napoleon Hill

January 1975, Homestead, California

Steven Jobs and Steve Wozniak couldn't believe their eyes!

There, on the front cover of the January edition of *Popular Electronics* magazine was a color photograph of the Altair 8800, the world's first micro-computer!

Up to that point, the only "real" computers in the world were huge, multi-million-dollar mainframes owned by the government, major universities, and big businesses. Only engineers with high security clearance could get near a computer back in 1975.

But that was about to change.

The two recent high school graduates stared at the cover of *Popular Electronics* magazine. They read and re-read the article on the Altair 8800 before arriving at a landmark decision — they would build a microcomputer that was better looking and easier to use than this one!

Wozniak worked evenings in Jobs' garage to build, in his words, "a personal computer I wanted for myself."

The Total Techie and the Big Dreamer

Wozniak was a classic computer nerd. A "total techie." He loved reading books on electronics. He loved figuring out how to design and build electronic gadgets, like radios, calculators, and computers. His dream was to build a personal computer, or PC, as it was later called, that he could fool around with at home and show off to a few friends.

Jobs, on the other hand, was a visionary. Although only 19 years old at the time, he saw their PC project as more than a hobby. He saw the PC as a potential business.

"My dream for the Apple II computer was to sell the first real packaged computer [containing a monitor and keyboard]," he said. "My dream was to sell 1,000 computers a month."

When the Apple II debuted in 1978, it was an instant success, and the two young partners were on their way to becoming multi-millionaires. Because Jobs accomplished his dream of selling 1,000 Apple II computers a month so quickly, he realized he needed a bigger dream (even though selling 1,000 computers a month in 1978 *when the PC industry didn't even exist* was a HUGE dream!).

Jobs never again made the mistake of dreaming too small. His new, improved dream was to do his part to place a PC on every desk in every home, school, and office in the world. Wow!... talk about a big dream!

Can you imagine trying to sell people on this dream in 1978 when there were more million-dollar mainframe computers than PCs in the world? But Jobs' dream wasn't that far-fetched. In fact, Jobs may live long enough to see his dream come true!

According to Michael Murphy, editor of *Technology Investing* newsletter, "There are 330 million personal computers in use today, and there are likely to be 10 times as many installed 10 years from now." Who could have predicted that in the span of only two decades the personal computer would totally transform the world economy?

And to think it all started with a dream of selling 1,000 computers a month! Amazing!

Big Dreams Create Big Results

What do you think would have happened if Jobs, back in 1977, had bought into Wozniak's dream of building one computer to fool around with as a hobby, instead of the other way around? Do you think the computer industry would be where it is today?... or the economy?... or the world, for that matter?

Not a chance!

But because Steven Jobs had the vision and courage to dream a big dream, he got big, BIG results... and as a result, millions of people all over the world have access to powerful, affordable computers. Jobs' big dream not only created a mega-industry —it revolutionized the way the world lives and works. Jobs is proof that big dreams create big results. Little dreams produce little results. And no dreams? You guessed it — no results!

Napoleon Hill, author of *Think and Grow Rich*, uses a wonderful metaphor to describe the importance of dreams in our lives. He says, "A dream is a blueprint for your ultimate achievements."

Isn't that a wonderful way of putting it? When you think about it, we're all architects of our own lives, aren't we? We draw up our blueprints with our dreams... and then we set about building those dreams. It stands to reason that you can't build a mansion with mobile-home-size dreams. Like I said, little dreams produce little results.

What About Your Dreams?

What about the size of your dreams? Are you reaching for big dreams, like young Steven Jobs? Or are you settling for little dreams, like young Steve Wozniak?

Do you have big dreams so that you can enjoy big results? Or are you limiting the size of your achievements by having small dreams?

Is your dream to own a mansion?... or to rent a one-bedroom apartment?

Is your dream to send your children to a top-notch university?... or to the local junior college while they live at home?

Is your dream to own your own high-profit business?... or to work at a company where you do the work while your boss gets the credit (and the raises)?

Maybe you have big dreams for your life. If you do, you're an exception, that's for sure. It's been my experience that most people settle for drawing up low-budget, mediocre-dream blueprints for their lives. Why? I think it's because the vast majority of people live their lives backward — they let their income decide the size of their dreams instead of allowing *their dreams to determine the size of their income!*

If more people would dream bigger dreams, they'd be looking for *opportunities* to create more wealth in their lives, instead of budgeting their money... budgeting their talents... budgeting their ambitions... and budgeting their potential.

In the words of Eleanor Roosevelt, *"The future belongs to those who believe in the beauty of their dreams."*

I challenge you to dream big dreams and then to open your mind to the information you're about to read in the coming pages. I challenge you to think out of the box... to do some dot.com dreaming... and then to believe in the beauty of those dreams.

For if you do, *the future will belong to you!*

...3...

Will You Take Advantage of Change?... (or Will You Let Change Take Advantage of You?)

Anytime there is change, there is opportunity. So it is paramount that an organization get energized rather than paralyzed.

—Jack Welch, CEO, General Electric

Where there is life, there is change. Just look at how much you've changed over the years.

Do you wear the same type of clothes as you did when you were 16?

How about your hairstyle — has it changed?

Are you still living with your parents?

Do you listen to the same music?... drive the same car?... hang out with the same friends?... attend the same high school?

Of course not!

You've grown, haven't you? You've moved on.

In other words, *you've changed!*

I'm reminding you of the obvious to bring home a point. Change is a fact of life. Change isn't bad. It's not something to be avoided. Change is something to be embraced, because periods of great change are also periods of great opportunity.

Inventions That Changed Our Paradigms

Nowadays we often hear the phrase "paradigm shift" to describe what happens when people alter their belief systems to accommodate dramatic changes in their lives. The word *paradigm* means "a model or a point of view." Paradigms are the thought patterns containing our beliefs — they represent the way we see the world and our role in it.

During the 20th century, there have been dozens of major paradigm shifts, and they were usually precipitated by breakthrough inventions that forced people to adapt to change, as was the case with the electric light bulb... the telephone... the movies... radio and TV... and commercial flight, to name a few.

Each of these paradigm-shifting inventions ushered in periods of great change... accompanied by great opportunity. Some of the biggest, most profitable companies in the world today were originally formed to exploit breakthrough inventions that occurred more than 100 years ago, such as General Electric and Bell Telephone.

Paradigm Shifts vs. Civilization Shifts

Of the dozens of breakthrough inventions of the 20th century, there are two that did more than shift some long-held paradigms — *they shattered them!* We're not just talking paradigm shifts here — we're talking *civilization shifts!* The inventions I'm talking about — the automobile and the personal computer — did more than change the world. *They turned the world upside down and shook it like a child shaking a rag doll!* Let's take a moment to discuss the civilization-altering impact of these two mass-produced inventions, starting with the automobile.

More than any other invention, the automobile shifted the Industrial Age into high gear and revved up the world economy. Cities expanded outward. New housing developments sprang up. New jobs were created.

As the economy grew by leaps and bounds, so did the dreams of millions of workers around the world. And what they dreamed about most was owning their own car! By 1928, only 25 years after Henry Ford founded the Ford Motor Company, there were 20 million cars in America, over half of them Model T Fords. To accommodate the growing traffic, thousands of workers built a massive network of roads... bridges... and highways connecting coast to coast in North America and country to country throughout Europe and Asia.

Entire industries and giant corporations came of age as a result of the automobile, and famous industrialists made vast fortunes supplying raw materials to build America's growing demand for cars — Rockefeller in oil... Carnegie and Morgan in steel... Firestone in rubber.

The automobile changed the world for the better, that's for certain. Within a few short decades, millions of people had more wealth... owned more things... and had more choices than they had ever dreamed possible.

PCs: The Automobile of the Information Age

What the automobile was to the Industrial Age, the PC is to the Information Age. Affordable PCs are the Model T of the Information Age, and the Internet is the "information superhighway."

As the Information Age shifts into high gear, change (and the opportunities that go with it) are occurring at mind-boggling speed and frequency. The Internet is not just about "Junior" sitting in his college dorm room e-mailing Mom and Dad for more money, anymore than the automobile was just about the family going for a drive after church. That's only a small piece of a pie that's the size of the globe!

Remember, we're talking about civilization shifts here! The automobile was only the beginning of bigger things to come. First the automobile... then highways... then commercial jet travel... then moon landings and space exploration.

The same goes for the PC — there are bigger things to come — MUCH BIGGER! The Internet "superhighway" is just being built! Right now there are a few shopping centers and strip malls popping up here and there along the e-highway. But the Wal-Marts of the Internet are still under construction. Which means there are plenty of BIG OPPORTUNITIES TO GO ALONG WITH THE BIG CHANGES TAKING PLACE.

Let me ask you a question: Knowing what you know today, how would you have liked to have been an investor in Wal-Mart before Sam Walton took his company public? How would you like to have been one of the first franchisees of McDonald's... or Holiday Inn... when the initial investment cost a few thousand dollars instead of a few hundred thousand? You'd be sittin' pretty right now, wouldn't you? And all because you embraced change and took advantage of it, instead of ignoring it.

"Who Moved My Cheese?"

The long and short of it is that change is a fact of life. The question isn't, "I wonder when things will stop changing so much?" Wrong question. The question is, "How will I deal with change?" *Will I take advantage of change.. or will I let change take advantage of me?*

There's a great little book called *Who Moved My Cheese?* by Spencer Johnson, M.D., that teaches us some valuable lessons about change and how to deal with it. If you haven't read *Who Moved my Cheese?*, I suggest you run to your local bookstore and buy a copy (or pull up your favorite dot.com bookstore and order one). The book is a short parable that can be read in less than an hour, but believe me, it could have a big, BIG impact on your life!

Who Moved My Cheese? is the delightful story of two "littlepeople" named Hee and Haw and two mice named Sniff and Scurry who live and work in a maze. Each morning they run through the maze to a room containing their cheese, where they eat until it's time to return home. Life is good, and everyone is happy and content.

But then one day the unthinkable happens — SOMEONE MOVES THEIR CHEESE! The rest of the story is about their search for new cheese and the emotional impact that the moved cheese has on each of their lives.

Adapting to Change

There are many wonderful lessons to learn from *Who Moved My Cheese?*, and the cheese can symbolize different things to different people. But the main message I got from the book is that today, more than ever, our "cheese" — that is, the way we earn money and support our dreams — is being moved, whether we like it or not. When our supply of cheese starts to dwindle… or if we wake up one morning and the cheese is gone because we've been fired or "down-sized," we have to head out into the maze and find another room that has some cheese.

The most interesting part of the parable to me was how each of the characters responded to the cheese being moved. As soon as the two mice discovered their cheese was gone, they did what came naturally — they immediately went in search of new cheese.

But the littlepeople had a tougher time adapting to change. First they denied that the cheese had been moved. They kept going back to the room even though the cheese was no longer there. Then Hem decided that he could bring the cheese back by working harder. So he started earlier and worked later, knocking holes in the walls hoping to find hidden cheese.

Still no cheese. Then he got angry and blamed others for taking the cheese that was rightfully his! He blamed the government. He blamed his parents. But that didn't bring the cheese back, either. Finally, out of desperation, Hem and Haw ventured into the maze in search of more cheese — but only as a last resort!

Do You See Yourself in This Parable?

Do any of the lessons in this parable hit home? Do you see parallels to your own life when I talk about Hem and Haw going into denial about obvious changes in their lives?... or getting angry when their "cheese entitlement" is taken from them?... or working harder in their old cheese room, hoping that will produce more cheese?

Well, like it or not, more than ever before in history, we're cast adrift in a stormy sea of change. And we're faced with a choice: We can either risk our lives by trying to sail against the relentless wind in an effort to get back to a familiar port. Or we can sail with the wind until we find a new port.

The famous economist Lester C. Thurow summed it up this way:

> *A competitive world has two possibilities.*
> *You can lose. Or if you want to win, you*
> *can change.*

I know you don't want to "lose," whether it's your cheese or your security or your paycheck. I don't either. But adapting to change doesn't mean you have to lose. You can win... and win BIG... by taking advantage of change. The simple truth is that ages of great change are also ages of great opportunity and tremendous wealth creation. The people who have recognized these changes and positioned themselves to profit from them have been able to create huge fortunes.

Internet Age: More Change... Faster Change... Bigger Change

Today we are entering the *Internet Age — an age that will propel the Information Age into hyper-drive!* The people who make fortunes in the Internet Age will be the ones who can capitalize on the digital distribution of information and/or products to the hundreds of millions of people (soon to be billions) who are interconnected via a global network of PCs. And believe me, the wealth created via the Internet Age will far surpass the wealth of the three previous ages combined!

How do I know? Because it's already happening.

In the Internet Age, change occurs monthly, even daily, as information is zapped around the world at the speed of light. In the Internet Age, our cheese is not only being moved — it's being tossed around like a softball at the annual company picnic. Flexible people who embrace change as a way of life will position themselves to profit at the speed of light.

Changing of the Guard

The Internet is changing the way the old companies conduct business in new the new e-economy, that's for sure! For example, IBM announced it would offer its entire PC product line for sale over the Internet — just like their rivals Dell, Gateway, and Compaq had been doing. Why? Because Internet sales had moved IBM's cheese, that's why! They've been losing money trying to sell their computers using the old distribution model, and they were forced to enter the Internet Age or get left in the cyber-dust.

Even Barbie is getting the message! The Barbie doll is the top-selling toy of all time. Mattel has sold *billions of Barbies* through retail stores since she was first introduced in 1959. So how did Mattel celebrate her 40th birthday in April of 1999? The world's biggest toy-maker announced it would cut 3,000 jobs and invest $50 million to build an Internet unit. The Internet moved Barbie's cheese — *and she wants it back!*

Same thing with the major car manufacturers. Ford and GM have launched online buying services, and *MoneyWorld* magazine reports that "Individuals who are already involved in the Internet car-buying service believe that 60% to 75% of buying activity will happen online in the next three years."

Blue Chips Give Way to Computer Chips

Can you guess the name of the person that CEOs of the Old Economy companies, such as Ford, are asking to meet with? According to a *USA Today* article, the "old guard" is most after advice from Michael Dell, CEO of Dell Computer, who, at 34, is younger than most children of the average Fortune 500 CEO!

Why Dell? Because Dell Computer has online sales of $14 million EACH DAY... and Dell's earnings have grown at an annual rate of 40% over the last three years! Those kind of numbers will make the oldest of the old guard take a new look at e-commerce.

A 1999 *Fortune* magazine article stated that "1998 will likely signal the beginning of the end" of the dominance of the old "blue chip" Industrial Age companies, such as General Motors and Coca-Cola, both of which have been around for over a century. Younger Internet Age companies, such as Dell computers, Microsoft, and Cisco (makers of Internet switching devices) "are wielding more influence in corporate America," *Fortune* said.

Where Do You Start Looking for Cheese?

Okay, assuming you're not a total techie whiz kid like Michael Dell... Bill Gates... or Jeff Bezos, where do YOU start looking for new cheese?

The best way to answer that question is to explain the secret to accumulating a huge storehouse of cheese, a concept commonly known as "wealth creation." It's a secret as old as mankind itself, and this is one secret that holds true for every age of dramatic change, the Internet Age included.

Wouldn't it be great to be in a position not to have to worry about your cheese being moved all the time?

Well, it stands to reason that if you understand the secret to making your own cheese... then you won't have to worry about someone else moving your cheese all the time, wouldn't you agree?

That's what the next chapter is about — the one enduring secret behind every great fortune that has ever been made... the secret that could empower you to become the next dot.com dream come true!

...4...

"So, What's The Secret Of The Wealthy, Anyway?"

"I've been rich and I've been poor. Rich is better."

–Sophie Tucker

J oe Louis, the great heavyweight boxing champion, summed up the benefits of wealth with this simple but profound statement:

"I don't like money, actually. But it quiets my nerves."

Isn't that a great line? And there's a lot of truth to it. Money does quiet the nerves by freeing us from the stresses and strains that come from having "too much month at the end of the money."

Louis understood that money isn't an end in itself. It's only a *means* to an end. What we're really after isn't money. Money is just paper. What we're really after is the *benefits of money*, that is, what money can buy. And more than anything else, money can buy freedom, starting with freedom from financial worries. Here's a partial list of some more freedoms that money can buy:

Freedom to come and go as you please.

Freedom to send your children to top-notch schools.

Freedom to live in the neighborhood of your choice (instead of the neighborhood you can *most* afford).

Freedom to take long vacations without worrying about how you're going to pay the credit card bills when you get back home.

Most of all, freedom to close the "dream gap"… to live big dreams. Yep, I'd say money quiets the nerves, all right.

Now, don't get me wrong. There are a lot of things in this life more important than money to me, such as my family. I'm not saying money is the key to happiness. But I am saying that the more money you have, the easier it is to get the key made!

The Get-a-Job Mentality

If money is so important, why don't more people have more of it?

Good question.

I think a big part of the reason is that people don't fully understand how wealth is created. They think the get-a-job formula is the only viable way to create wealth because, well, because that's the formula they've been taught since they were kids.

Over the years we've been conditioned to accept the get-a-job mentality. Our parents had *full-time jobs.* Our friends had *part-time jobs.* The school counselors encouraged us to attend *job fairs...* showed us how to fill out *job applications...* coached us on what to say during a *job interview.* Is it any wonder so many people get conditioned to think of a job as the only way to create wealth?

The job certainly is one way for people to create wealth. But it's not the *only way.* Fact is, it's never been a very *powerful way.* And today, it's not even a very *dependable way* to create wealth!

No More Job Security

Only a few years ago you could at least expect *some* job security. Your job may not have paid a lot, but you knew you could count on it being there, year in and year out.

Then, during the '80s, the deal changed. Job security started disappearing. The corporations said the recession was forcing them to "downsize," as they called it. But when the economy got better in the '90s, the downsizing didn't stop — and it still hasn't stopped!

In 1998, despite record-setting profits, corporate America eliminated 600,000 jobs. That's right — they swept 600,000 jobs out the door like they were something the boss' kids tracked in. Same thing is going on in Europe... Australia... Asia. Corporations are pumping up their profit sheets by cutting back on the payroll.

Climbing the Corporate Pyramid

It's always been tough for employees to advance up the corporate pyramid. But millions of bright, ambitious people still sign up to play a game I call "Climbing the Corporate Pyramid." The game goes like this:

You start at the bottom and work hard. You move up a little, so you work even harder. When you become really successful, what happens? You out-perform your supervisor. So he makes sure you get shuffled around or held down so you don't threaten his position. No matter what level you're at, there's always a cap on your income. Because despite what *YOU are worth*, you'll never be paid more than what *the JOB is worth*.

The closer you get to the top of the pyramid, the less room there is. No wonder it's lonely at the top — there just isn't much room up there to begin with.

And it's only a matter of time before you reach your plateau, because no matter how good you are, the closer you get to the top, the fewer jobs there are, as evidenced by the illustration below:

THE BIGGEST PYRAMID
Traditional Corporate Structure

One CEO

Several Regional Managers

Many District Managers

Thousands of Sales Representatives

This simple illustration reminds me of the rough-and-tumble child's game, "King of the Hill," where one of the neighborhood kids would climb to the top of a hill and then shove the other kids who dared challenge his throne, sending them tumbling to the bottom. Some kids just never grow up, I guess.

From Bad to Worse

Climbing the Corporate Ladder used to have its perks. You may not have become the King of the Hill, but at least you were in the king's court. You had a key to the executive restroom. You had a corner office. And your high-paying, high-status job was secure.

But that was then, and this is now.

"FINISHED AT FORTY!" screams the headline on the cover of *Fortune* magazine. The lead article paints a dark portrait of the corporate pyramid, a portrait that will only get darker with time.

"The older an employee, the more likely it is he [or she] can be replaced by someone younger who earns half as much," states *Fortune*. "Middle managers can't rise to the top (there's no room). In years gone by, executives in this position spoke of reaching a plateau — if their path no longer led upward, at least they were in a stable, safe place. Now the plateau is a narrow ledge."

Government statistics confirm that workers are being pushed off the "narrow ledge" with increasing frequency. According to the U.S. Census Bureau, the average worker in the U.S. will have 10 to 12 different jobs in four to five different career areas during their lives — which means they'll be changing jobs every four to five years. Where's the security in that?

Income Gap Gets Wider by the Day

How can someone create significant, lasting wealth if they're starting over every few years? No wonder more than two million Americans filed for bankruptcy last year. Just when they start to move up, they're forced to move out.

We talked about the income gap earlier — it's the gap between the haves and the have-nots. And it's getting wider by the day. Business writer Gene Marlow says that nearly 20 years ago it took a CEO a week to match his worker's salary. Not so today.

"CEOs make in one day," Marlowe writes, "what workers take a year to earn."

Corporate America isn't just moving our cheese — they're stealing our cheese and then hoarding it in their corner offices. "Less for you, more for me," is their motto.

Enough, already! It's time to take things into our own hands... to take control of our lives... to own our own cheese-making operations so that we don't have to settle for handouts anymore.

Secret of the Wealthy

So, if a job isn't the best way to create wealth, what is? What do wealthy people do that enables them to create far more wealth than the average person? Well, before I answer that, let me add that the secret of the wealthy has been around since the beginning of time.

The secret of the wealthy is immutable, which means it will never become old-fashioned or go out of favor, no matter how fast or how much the world changes. The secret of the wealthy is written in stone. And it's the key to every great fortune ever made.

So, what is the secret of the wealthy, anyway?

I can answer that question in two words — *they own.*

They own their own businesses. They own stocks in other companies. They own their own homes. They own their own lives. And they own their own dreams. You see, wealthy people understand that when you're an independent business owner, you're building *your dream*, not someone else's.

Little Money, Big Dreams

One of the biggest myths about becoming an independent business owner is this oft-repeated cliche: "It takes money to make money." I always hear this excuse from people who are looking for reasons *not* to become independent business owners.

Well, lack of money has never been a valid excuse for not starting a successful business, especially today, when high-powered technology is so readily available and inexpensive. Just take a look at some of these Information Age success stories that were started on a shoestring. All of these startups, by the way, became multi-billion-dollar companies:

Original Investments to Start Five Computer Companies

Hewlett-Packard ....started with $538

Apple Computer ......started with $1,600
(Steven Jobs sold his VW van)

Oracle Systems ....started with $1,500

Compaq.....................started with $3,000

Gateway 2000............started with $10,000
(borrowed from a founder's mom)

The success of these five companies proves that you don't have to have a huge capital outlay to start and build a large, profitable business. When it comes to starting a business, the size of your bank account is secondary to the size of your dream and the size of your heart!

The founders of these six companies recognized that the world was undergoing massive paradigm shifts, which in turn were creating massive opportunities. The founders were in the right place at the right time, but then so were millions of other people. The difference is that David Packard, Bill Hewlett, and the others had the smarts to recognize a great opportunity when they saw one. And they had the wisdom to understood that owning your own business is the only way to fly.

Look, all of these guys were brilliant. They could have gotten high-paying jobs with any one of a dozen companies. But they understood the power of ownership. They understood that ownership means freedom. Ownership means building your own dream and calling your own shots. And ownership means unlimited opportunity.

Your New Business in the e-Economy

I'm not so naive as to think that you're going to start the next Apple Computer Company for a few thousand dollars. Let's face it, every single one of the founders of the above companies was super-smart to the "n^{th}" degree. I'm nowhere near their league in brain power, and, more than likely, neither are you.

But that's one of the great things about the e-economy — you don't have to be super-rich or super-smart to build your dream business.

All you have to do is recognize that you're in the right place at the right time... and then be willing to take advantage of the greatest economic revolution in history.

Part Two

What Would Your Dream Business Look Like?

···5···

What Would Your Dream Business Look Like?

Go confidently in the direction of your dreams. Live the life you've imagined.
—Henry David Thoreau

It was 1987. I was 24 years old and had just completed my first year selling cellular phones. I was making good money, but I was tired of building someone else's dream.

It was time to build my own dream.

So I opened what I thought was my dream business, a cellular phone store in Clearwater, Florida.

It didn't take long for my dream business to turn into a nightmare business. Have you ever heard the statistic that 80% of small businesses go out of business within the first year? Well, I was one of those 80% — I didn't make it past the first year! In my seminars, I tell people that by age 25, I had earned a million dollars — but it cost me $1.2 million to earn it!

Here's what happened.

One Nightmare after the Other

I was pretty proud the day we opened the doors. I had a 3,000-square-foot retail store on the busiest street in Clearwater, Florida. The aisles and walls were lined with $200,000 worth of inventory. I hired a receptionist, and I personally trained all 10 of the sales reps. The accountant had his own office, right next to mine so I could keep an eye on the books. I hired a crackerjack service manager and a couple of inexperienced technicians who I prayed would learn quickly on the job. I ran some big splashy ads in the newspaper. Hung a banner across the door. And waited for the money to come pouring in.

It poured, all right, as in, "When it rains, it pours!"

It didn't take long for reality to set in. Each month I had to ring up $100,000 in sales just to keep the doors open. Every time I turned around, the accountant was standing there holding a pen and the company checkbook.

"Sign here," he'd say. I signed there. And I signed... and signed... and signed. Meanwhile, new inventory had to be ordered... old inventory paid for... and yet another new employee hired. "Can you give me a two-week advance?" he asked sweetly. Innocently, I signed another check. I never saw the guy again.

I personally trained 30 different sales people in 11 months. Most of them, however, didn't earn their salaries in commissions. The only two good ones I ever had quit and opened their own stores down the street. My operations manager slipped off her chair and hurt her back. Workers' Compensation insurance paid for her back operation. It didn't pay for my attorney, however, when she hauled me into court.

To meet payroll, I went months without paying myself. I even took advances against my credit cards to make payroll. The employees got the money, I got the debt. The bills kept coming in. The employees kept walking out. And I kept getting deeper and deeper in debt. American Express told me to leave home without it!

Expensive but Valuable Lessons

Yep, opening up my dream business was the second-best decision I made in 1987. The best decision I made that year was to close my nightmare business down!

They say experience is the best teacher. If that's true, then I earned my Ph.D. in Business Administration in less than a year! I learned some valuable lessons, no doubt about that. Expensive lessons, but valuable ones. And as a result, I've been able to avoid some costly errors in later businesses.

I tell you this story to illustrate a crucial point. Just because you dream about opening a business doesn't make it a dream business! In other words, not all businesses are created equal, believe me! Some businesses are better than other businesses, and that's a fact!

Characteristics of a Dream Business

I took a few minutes and jotted down a few characteristics of a dream business versus a traditional business. When you compare them side by side, it's easy to see that owning a dream business would be a lot more attractive than owning a traditional business.

OWNING A DREAM BUSINESS	VS.	OWNING A TRADITIONAL BUSINESS
No employees		Employees
Set your own hours		9 a.m.to 9 p.m., six days a week
Low start-up cost		All your savings plus bank loans
No restrictions on territory		Limited territory
Experienced mentors to advise you		On your own
Unlimited Income		Income limited by number of stores
Recession-proof		Dependent on seasons or economy
Low inventory		Inventory is biggest expense
Low overhead		Monthly lease plus utilities
No advertising		Expensive advertising budget
Residual income		Trade time for dollars

As you can see, there's a big difference between a dream business and the realities of a traditional business. As you look over the list, you might be thinking, "Hey, if there really were a business that had all of the advantages of a dream business and none of the disadvantages of a traditional business, I'd be foolish not to give it a serious look."

My thoughts exactly. Well, as you'll discover, there is such a dream business. It has all of the traits listed above, plus a few others that we'll discuss shortly.

Five Criteria for a Dream Business

Over the years I've become a real student of business. I've founded, owned, and operated more than a dozen businesses since my cellular phone fiasco. I've talked to hundreds of successful businesspeople representing scores of profitable businesses. I've read business books... listened to business tapes... and attended business seminars.

I took all that information and boiled it down to the essential ingredients of a dream business. What I came up with are five criteria that a business must meet in order to be classified as a true "dream business." They are as follows:

Five Criteria for a Dream Business

1) *Residual Income*
   (you do the work once, get paid again and again)

2) *Global Market*

3) *Willable and Sellable*

4) *Duplicatable*
   (cookie-cutter system that can be repeated over and over)

5) *Low Investment and Low Maintenance*
   (home-based would be ideal)

If you can find a business that meets ALL of these criteria, you've got a sure winner. But keep in mind that a *true dream business must meet all five criteria.* If the business meets four of the five, that's not enough because in the end, it will be just another traditional business with a few dream business traits.

It's like dialing a phone number — if you miss one of the numbers, you miss your connection. You have to key in each of the numbers in the right sequence to achieve the results you want. Same goes for your dream business. If you miss even one of the above criteria, you'll make the wrong connection.

What About Professionals?

I get the impression that most people feel that professionals — people like doctors, lawyers, and accountants — enjoy the ultimate dream business.

They earn lots of money. They have lots of status. Live the life of Riley, so to speak.

But when you talk to professionals, you get a different story. Doctors, for example, have tremendous overhead, what with offices and high-tech equipment. The hours are horrendous, and the malpractice insurance takes a big chunk of their gross income. To complicate matters, HMOs keep lowering doctors' fees, so that only the top specialists are able to command six-figure incomes anymore.

When you look at the criteria for a dream business, the only one that doctors meet is number three — some doctors and dentists are able to sell their practices when they retire.

"What about those doctors and attorneys who earn $250 or more an hour?" you might ask. "If that's not a dream business, I can still live with it!" True, many professionals earn huge hourly wages. But the downside of that is they have to keep going back into the salt mines, grinding out those "billable hours." If they become sick or disabled, the hours don't get billed, and the professionals don't get paid. The credo for professionals is "No hours... No paycheck... No excuses!"

The biggest downside to being a professional is that your income is linear instead of residual. In other words, they get paid one hour's wages for one hour's work. If they want to earn more, they have to put in more hours. And let's face it, there are only so many hours you can work a day without losing your sanity... or your health... or your family... or all three!

The beauty of residual income is that you do the work once and you get paid for that work over and over again. That's why pop singers like Elton John or movie directors like Steven Spielberg are able to amass huge fortunes. It may only take Elton John 20 minutes to write a song that earns him millions of dollars in royalties, year in and year out. Time does not equate to money when it comes to royalties. All that counts is whether or not people like his songs well enough to plunk down $15 or more for his CDs.

Do you have any idea how much Elvis Presley earns in residual income each year? According to *Forbes* magazine, Elvis earned $35 million in royalties in 1998 alone — and he's been dead for more than 20 years!

Do you know any attorneys or doctors who would be willing to trade their big hourly fee for one of Elton John's or Elvis Presley's hit songs that took 20 minutes to write? I think we both know the answer to that!

What About Franchising?

More and more people are turning to franchising as a dream business. And there's no question that franchising has some huge advantages over tradi- tional mom-and-pop operations. For one thing, franchisees buy into a proven, turnkey system. They don't have to reinvent the wheel. They just have to learn the system and connect the dots. Franchising meets criteria number four in that it's a duplicatable system. It's also willable and sellable. Those are some big pluses in the franchising column.

But there are some big minuses, too. For one thing, the average franchise fee approaches $50,000 — and the cost keeps going up. To buy into one of the top franchise systems, such as McDonald's, that figure is closer to a million dollars. And what do you get for that investment? You get, well, *you get a job!*

That's right, you get the privilege of working six or seven days a week, from nine in the morning to nine at night. Then each month you cut a check totaling 6% to 9% of your gross profits to the parent company for the privilege of using their system and brand name. If you work a six-day week and watch the cash register closely, you can make $50,000, maybe as much as $100,000, a year from a busy franchise. But as everyone in the franchising industry knows, you don't make the really big, BIG bucks until you own multiple franchises. So much for low cost and low maintenance, eh?

Hey, I'm not saying that franchising is a bad deal. It's certainly a much better way to run a business than making it up as you go along. All I'm saying is that a franchise isn't a dream business. Franchisees are restricted to certain territories... they have to manage an army of unskilled, unmotivated, under-achieving employees... and the start-up fees and overhead are killer! Franchises are a great deal for the franchisor because he gets residual income... and he gets access to a global market. But let's get real here, how many people do you know who have the savvy to start their own franchise system? For the average person like you or me, it's just not a realistic alternative.

You Can't Make a Porsche Out of a VW

Some people go to great lengths to make their traditional business perform like a dream business. They work harder, putting in impossibly long hours so that their business will earn them more income. Maybe they try to lure more customers into their store by making obnoxious TV commercials, like those automobile dealership commercials featuring a screaming pitchman wearing a cheap suit.

Yes, hard work and effective advertising can make a traditional business more profitable. But as I always say, either way you pay. And there's a steep price to pay for working long hours and running expensive ads.

When people try "tricks" to turn a traditional business into a dream business, it reminds me of the story that Steven Jobs likes to tell about a childhood friend who owned a Volkswagen Bug. The friend really wanted to make his Bug a Porsche. So he spent all his spare money and time accessorizing his VW, making it look and sound loud. By the time he was done, he'd spent thousands of dollars and hundreds of hours on his VW.

But he still didn't have a Porsche. *He had a loud, ugly VW bug!*

Jobs says the point of the story is that you've got to be careful choosing what you're going to do with your time and money. You can't turn a VW into your dream vehicle no matter how hard you try. You'll just waste your money and your time trying.

Likewise, you can't turn a job into a high-performance, wealth-creating vehicle anymore than Steven Job's childhood friend could turn his VW Bug into a Porsche. If you're serious about building a high-performance wealth-creating vehicle, then you need to start with a vehicle with high-performance potential — a vehicle that meets ALL of the criteria of a true dream business!

Ignorance Is Just a Lack of Education

When I opened up my nightmare cellular phone business, I thought I was opening my dream business. My expectations were way out of line with reality. Why? Because I was ignorant.

Now, when I use the word "ignorant," I don't mean to imply I was stupid. Or that I lacked the ability to make a business work. When I say I was ignorant, I mean *I lacked education.* I didn't have all the information I needed to make good decisions. I was in the dark, and when the bright light of reality came flooding in, I looked around and saw that what I thought was a dream business was really a nightmare.

I think ignorance is the reason so many people go into nightmare businesses. It's also the reason so many people try to turn their low-performance VW Bug-type businesses or VW Bug-type jobs into high-performance Porsches. They mean well. They just haven't been given the information that will help them understand the difference between a dream business and a nightmare business.

Once people understand the key elements to a dream business, they'll understand which opportunities to pursue… and which ones to turn down.

The Benefits of the Dream Business Criteria

I've been saying all along that money isn't what people are *really* after — it's the *benefits* of money they really want. Likewise, becoming an independent business owner of a dream business isn't what people are really after — it's the *benefits of a successful business* that people really want.

With that in mind, let's take a brief look at each of the Dream Business criteria again and discuss the BENEFITS of those criteria.

Criterion 1: Residual Income

Wouldn't it be great to do the work once and then have it pay you over and over again? That's what residual income is all about. A classic example is investing in the stock market. Let's say it takes you 100 hours of work at your job to earn $1,000. To earn $100,000 using the time-for-dollars formula, you'd have to work 10,000 hours at $10 per hour, which would calculate to working 40 hours a week for almost five years.

But if you invested that $1,000 one time in a high-return stock, it would continue to earn money for you year after year. For example, if you had purchased $1,000 of Warren Buffett's Berkshire stock in 1965 when it first debuted, how much do you think it would be worth today? $10,000, maybe? $100,000? Try $1,989,526! That's right — almost $2 million bucks on a $1,000 investment.

This enormous return on investment is the result of a concept called compounding or exponential growth, which we'll discuss in a moment. But compounding and residual income are both examples of what happens when you escape the time-for-money trap — you do the work once, and it keeps paying and paying, over and over again!

Criterion 2: Global Market

We live in a global village today. We can take an order from Australia on a Monday and have it in a customer's hands by Friday. So why settle for a niche market or a postage-stamp territory when the whole world can be at your fingertips? Big companies have understood this principle for years. That's why 60% of the Coca-Cola Company's business is overseas. It's also why McDonald's, Wendy's, and Pizza Hut are expanding much faster internationally than they are in the U.S. — there's a great, big, wonderful world out there, so we might as well sell to all of it instead of limiting our efforts to a tiny slice of a tiny pie.

Criterion 3: Sellable and Willable

It's not where you are right now that counts, but where you'll be in five years or 10 years from today. Making the decision to start your dream business is your first step to living your dreams. The second step is to plan your exit strategy in case you want to cash in or in case you're no longer able to work.

Wouldn't you sleep better if you knew your family and loved ones would be taken care of if something happened to you? Wouldn't you like to be in a position where your efforts were building equity at the same time they were generating income? A job will never be sellable or willable. A dream business must be both!

Criterion 4: Duplicatable System

If you want to be successful, it stands to reason that you need to do what successful people do. Likewise, if you want to build a successful dream business, you need to copy a successful business model.

Duplication isn't rocket science, folks. It's just good, old common sense. Successful mentors teach you their proven system for success. Once you learn the system and start getting results, you will, in turn, teach that proven system to your new partners... who will then teach it to their new partners... and so on down the line.

Like franchisees, independent business owners are in business FOR themselves, but not BY themselves. The organization's support system of books, tapes, live events, seminars, and one-on-one trainings will teach you the nuts and bolts of the business and steer you away from unproductive activities and toward proven, duplicatable strategies for building your business.

To ensure your dream business is successful, take a lesson from the king of franchises, McDonald's: *Keep it simple and keep it duplicatable.*

Criterion 5: Low Investment and Low Maintenance

Do you know the number one reason new businesses fail? They're undercapitalized. When you have to pay for expensive overhead while you're building a business, you just get further and further behind the eight ball. I know. It happened to me!

A dream business would have a low entry fee and low monthly maintenance. That means no employees. No big lease payments. No huge infrastructure requirements. No big inventory needs. No anything that rang up big monthly fixed expenses.

That's why home-based businesses make so much sense. It's a one-minute commute from your bedroom, and the overhead is zilch! You can install a high-powered, high-tech office in a spare bedroom — including computer and Internet service, scanner, fax, business phone, cell phone, and copier — for less than what it costs you to take your family to Walt Disney World for a weekend.

Leveraging Your Time with Technology

Hey, I've known people who built huge dream businesses from the kitchen table with a pencil, a notepad, and a phone, nothing else! But why make it hard on yourself? Just because you've "always done it that way" doesn't make it a better way.

It's like building a house. You can build a house a lot faster if you use a table saw instead of a hand saw. Likewise, you can build your dream business a lot faster if you use the high-tech tools available to you.

Let's face it, to take full advantage of the e-economy, you need access to the tools that drive that economy — a computer with Internet access. The Internet will help you build your dream business bigger and faster than you ever imagined.

How fast?

Maybe the title of Bill Gates' new book might give you a clue.

It's called *Business @ the Speed of Light.*

...6...

I Net, You Net, We All Net, The Internet!

> *If I had to name the one single attribute*
> *that defines the most successful people, it's*
> *their ability to network.*
>
> —Harvey Mackay, bestselling author & businessman

"*D*id you realize you're in the movie promotion business?" Tim Templeton, author of *Referral of a Lifetime*, asked me that question as we stood on the third tee of Old Memorial Golf Course in Tampa, Florida.

"What are you talking about?" I asked. His question came out of nowhere... right out of the blue.

One moment we were talking about networking, and the next moment he was asking me if I realized I was in the movie promotion business.

"We're all in the movie promotion business," Tim continued confidently. "When you see a good movie, what do you do? You tell your friends and family about it, don't you? You might even urge them to go see it — 'YOU GOTTA SEE THIS MOVIE! IT'S FANTASTIC!'

"You're in the movie promotion business. So am I," Tim continued. "So is everyone who goes to a movie and recommends it to friends. In fact, person-to-person promotion is the only way a movie can become a hit. The *only* way!

"Studios spend millions of dollars promoting some big-budget movie like *Godzilla*, and it turns out to be a box office dud. Then the same studio will allocate a bare-bones ad campaign to promote a low-budget movie like *Shakespeare in Love*, and it becomes a box office hit! What makes the difference? Person-to-person, word-of-mouth marketing. Nobody promoted the expensive dud, and everybody promoted the inexpensive hit.

"Hollywood calls it 'good buzz' when the word-of-mouth on a movie is positive," Tim continued. "When the buzz is negative, however, no amount of advertising can get people into the theater. Bad word-of-mouth is certain death. Good word-of-mouth is priceless. That's what I mean when I say you're in the movie promotion business. Interesting, isn't it?"

The Power of Networks

I've thought a lot about Tim's observation, and he's right on the money. We are in the movie promotion business. We're also in the restaurant promotion business. The doctor promotion business. The car promotion business. The vacation promotion business. The list goes on and on. We just don't get paid for it.

What's at work here is the power of networks. Anytime you have a group of individuals with a common interest and a method of sending and receiving information, you have a network. It's that simple.

The most basic network is our immediate family. Those are the people we see day in and day out. Another network is our business associates, people we work with daily. Then there are our networks at church... networks at school... networks of friends... networks in the neighborhood. You get the idea.

Each of our networks is connected to someone else's network, which is connected to other networks, and on and on, like a giant invisible constellation. I call these constellations of networks "internets" (with a small "i"), which is short for "inter-connected networks." Our personal internets are informal and unstructured, and they are amazingly efficient at sending and receiving information. In a matter of minutes or days, information — both good and bad — can be sent back and forth between dozens... or hundreds... or even thousands of people who have never met and who may be living almost anywhere in the world. Incredible!

How Networks Work

To better illustrate how our personal internets operate, let's return to the movie promotion analogy. Let's say you just saw a spectacular movie. It's fair to say you would recommend the movie to at least 10 people in your various networks. Let's assume those 10 people recommend it to 10 of their acquaintances ("I haven't seen it yet, but a guy in the office says it's great!") and so on. Here's how your personal internet would broadcast your information:

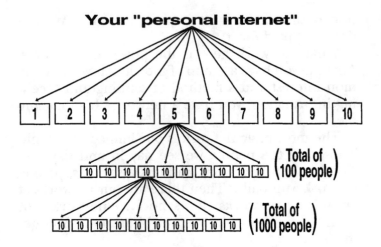

As you can see, within days hundreds of people could know about your endorsement. Within weeks and months, that number could multiply to thousands! This is a simplified illustration of how personal internets operate, but it gives you a pretty good idea of how far and how fast our personal internets can broadcast information. And it's the reason that word-of-mouth marketing is such an effective method of promotion.

As Natural as Breathing

Networking has been around since the first band of hunters and gatherers talked around a campfire thousands of years ago. Humans are social animals, and for us, networking is as natural as breathing. We start young and we continue networking all of our lives. As we become more adept and comfortable with networking, it becomes an indispensable part of our lives.

How did you choose your family doctor?... or lawyer?... or veterinarian? Perhaps you looked in the phone book. Perhaps you called for an appointment after seeing a TV commercial or newspaper ad. Perhaps. But if you're anything like me, you asked a trusted friend or business associate who suggested you go see so-and-so ("But whatever you do, *don't* go see SO-AND-SO!").

It's been my experience that people love to help. Everyone has an opinion, and they love to express it. And networking allows your friends and acquaintances to do both!

Human Internets vs. the Electronic Internet

Human networks grew larger and became more efficient as new communication technologies were introduced — first speech... then writing... then the telegraph... then the telephone... then the fax... and then the computer. Within a few short years of the invention of the personal computer, the concept of the small, personal internet (with a small "i") evolved into a colossal world-wide Internet (with a capital "I").

The difference between our low-tech personal internets and the high-tech global Internet is day and night. The basic principle of networking remains the same — people with common interests sharing information back and forth. But that's where the similarities end.

To say your personal internet is slow and small compared to the global Internet would be an understatement, to say the least! The difference between your personal *internet* and the global *Internet* is the difference between a bicycle and a Lear jet *in speed*... the difference between a book and the Library of Congress *in size*... the difference between a court jester and a king *in power*... and the difference between a phone call and a conference call *in inter-connectedness.*

Speed... size... power... and inter-connectedness — the Internet has enhanced and magnified all four of these networking traits to mind-boggling degrees. Like I said, the basic underlying principle of networking still applies. But instead of making one phone call and communicating with one member in your personal internet, with the Internet you can now send one e-mail and communicate with millions of members — and they can communicate back. The Internet is global networking at the speed of light.

Power to the People

Everyone who logs on soon realizes that the two most obvious advantages of the Internet are its speed and its size. *It's fast... and it's vast! You can reach millions in minutes!*

But there's another advantage of the Internet that most users overlook. I call the Internet the "Great Equalizer!" By that I mean that one computer is no better than any other computer. And one person is no better than any other person. The Internet doesn't care what you look like... whether you're young or old... whether you're white or black... whether you're a Ph.D. or a dropout — none of those things are an issue online unless you choose to make them an issue.

John Naisbitt, futurist and bestselling author, said it best: *"The bigger the world economy, the more powerful its smallest players."* Well, the world economy is big and getting bigger, thanks to the Internet.

And everyone online has equal power to buy, sell, inform, protest, complain, disagree, share, preach, whine, edify — you name it and you can do it on the Internet!

Because of the Internet, the "smallest players" — you and me and all the other "average Joes and Janes" out there — are, indeed, *more powerful than ever before!*

...7...

e-Commerce Is
e-Exploding!

The significance of the Internet CANNOT be overstated!

−Michael Eisner, Disney CEO to Disney shareholders

More people need to live their lives by the "Noah Principle."

"What's the Noah Principle?" you may ask.

The Noah Principle means *you don't get any prizes for predicting rain. You only get prizes for building the ark.* Our society has conditioned people to predict rain, that is, to complain about the problems but to ignore the solutions, especially if those solutions involve dreaming big dreams or thinking out of the box.

"Don't waste your time on foolish dreams," we're told. "Get real. Get your head out of the clouds. Get a job like everyone else."

Nonsense!

In the rest of this book, you're going to discover how to build your ark! You're going to discover the solution to the problems that so many people are facing today — lack of freedom, lack of money, and lack of a vehicle to accomplish their dreams. In short, you're going to discover how to design your future and live your dreams in the e-economy!

Let's get started by talking about the most amazing vehicle for wealth creation ever invented — the Internet — and how online shopping is revolutionizing the way people buy and sell products.

The Evolution of the Internet

The Internet got its start in 1969 when the Defense Department funded a project to link their computers with those of government research contractors, many of whom were working for universities. The experiment started small, connecting three computers in California with one in Utah.

By 1990, thousands of people in universities and government offices were using the Internet to communicate and exchange data. The Defense Department wisely decided it was time to make Internet technology available to the rest of the world.

The commercial Internet took a few years to gain momentum. In fact, in 1993, there were 130 websites on the entire Internet! But once the Internet caught on, websites began popping up like dandelions after a spring rain.

By 1999, there were millions of websites, and

some Internet experts are predicting there will be *100 million websites on the Internet by 2003!* Just think, the Internet is on track to grow from 130 websites to 100 million in 10 years! That's almost incomprehensible! WOW!

Internet Growth Continues to Explode

As I write this in 1999, the Internet is in the midst of an explosive growth phrase that should continue well into the New Millennium. But what's truly amazing is the astronomical rate of growth compared to other media.

Check this out: It took radio 38 years to reach 50 million listeners. It took TV 13 years to reach the 50-million mark. It only took the Internet four years to attract 50 million users! To give you some idea of how fast the Net is growing, there were more people online in 1999 than owned TV sets when Neil Armstrong first walked on the moon in 1969!

According to *Forbes* magazine, there were 150 million Internet users by the end of 1998 — half of them in the U.S. and Canada. Each day 15,000 people log onto the Internet for the first time. By 2001, as the Net becomes mainstream, analysts predict the number of Internet users will range from a low of 300 million people... to as many as 600 million! In *Star-Trek* language, the Internet is growing at warp speed!

What are people using the Internet for? A host of activities, including research... games... business-to-business marketing... chatting... support groups... downloading software... entertainment... communicating with friends... buying and selling goods and services... selling and bidding at auctions... advertising... education... and investing, among others.

The Biggest Uses of the Internet

By far the biggest use of the Internet right now is e-mail. The U.S. Postal Service delivers 330 million first class letters per day. E-mail far surpasses the number of letters delivered by "snail mail," as devotees of e-mail like to call the U.S. mail. As of June, 1998, there were more than a billion e-mail messages sent and received EACH DAY... A TRILLION EACH YEAR! And those numbers are expected to quadruple in the next few years!

Folks, I hope you're getting the message here. The Internet is not just a gimmick. It's not a toy for techno-geeks and computer nerds. It's here. It's now. And it's happening! To ignore it is not only unwise, it could well be suicide.

Oh, sure, you can get by without using the Internet. You can get by without learning to drive, too. You can get by without learning to read or write. But I wouldn't recommend any of those courses of action because they limit your potential!

Same with the Internet. John R. Levine, the author of *The Internet for Dummies*, puts it this way:

> *"This year [1999], we have to say the Internet is totally mainstream, and you're falling further behind the curve faster if you haven't gotten started."*

e-Commerce Is Coming on Strong!

One phenomenon that is drawing a lot of attention on Wall Street and in the media is online shopping, as well it should. Online shopping goes by several names — e-commerce and e-tailing being two of the most popular. But the one name that best describes e-commerce is *growth — massive, explosive growth!*

Right now e-commerce is doing somewhere between $10 and $20 billion a year... and it's in its infancy. But as the number of Internet users grows, e-commerce is sure to erupt like a pent-up volcano.

As I pointed out earlier, forecasts vary widely when it comes to predicting growth on the Internet. I've seen forecasts predicting a trillion dollars in sales on the Internet by 2005! But just to be on the safe side, let's stick to more conservative predictions for this section. Even the most conservative figures are still mind-boggling!

Morgan Stanley forecasts that e-commerce will grow at least 10-fold between the beginning of 1999 and the end of year 2000 — they predict it will end up somewhere between $21 billion and $56 billion per year.

By 2005, they predict that figure will jump to a whopping $115 billion a year! As I said, these are conservative growth figures.

Just look how steep the growth curve is on the graph below:

e-Commerce Revenues

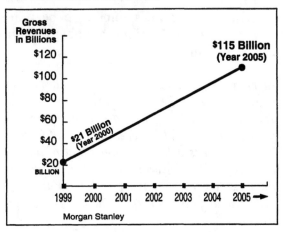

Take a moment to really think about these figures a bit. What these figures mean is that someone, or a whole bunch of someones, stand to make a mountain of money in the coming decade. By 2005, e-commerce could explode 50-fold to more than a

trillion! Folks, it's figures like these that make
Fortune 500 companies stand up and take notice.

Two Choices: Online... or Flatline

One-hundred-year-old Fortune 500 companies,
such as AT&T, are making billion-dollar deals left
and right, trying desperately to position themselves
for the e-commerce boom. They're throwing
money and stocks around like little kids trading
baseball cards. And if conservative, button-down
companies like AT&T are out in the marketplace
with an open checkbook, you KNOW THIS THING
IS FOR REAL!

"There's a game of musical chairs going on right
now," says Ethan Hopper, head of West Coast merg-
ers and acquisitions for Credit Suisse First Boston.
"The off-line companies realize they have to be
online or they are dead. This wave of consolidations
has just begun."

MoneyWorld magazine summed up beautifully the
enormous potential of online shopping with this common sense statement:

> *In many respects, the Internet is the ultimate retail
> superstore... open 24 hours a day, seven days a week.
> You never have to fight for a parking space. Aisles
> are not crowded with shoppers — even at Christmas.
> The selection is a hundred times that of the largest
> department store. Every product is in stock. Prices
> are low. There's no waiting in line. Purchases are
> delivered to your doorstep. The advantages go on
> and on.*

The biggest thing holding the e-commerce explosion back at this point is people's reluctance to give
out their credit card numbers over the Net. A recent
survey by Greenfield Online, Inc. reports that nearly
80% of consumers would do more shopping online
if they could be assured a company is reputable.

In other words, companies that have a name and reputation that people can trust will be positioned to profit in a big way through e-commerce in the New Millennium.

What's in It for Me?

It's hard to comprehend astronomical numbers like $115 billion a year by the year 2005. What does that really mean? Better yet, what does that really mean to *your pocketbook*, because, let's face it, we all want to know "What's in it for me?"

What's in it for you is the opportunity of a lifetime — the opportunity of all lifetimes, actually — because never before in history has the world seen an opportunity this size, this explosive, that is available to average people.

Historically, average people have never had access to the same wealth-creating tools as the rich. For centuries the kings owned all the land... the oil and steel tycoons owned all the raw materials... and the industrialists owned all the factories.

But the Internet leveled the playing field. It's the Great Equalizer. As Bill Gates says, "The Internet is a change agent, and it will reorder things." Right now it's reordering the way people shop... the way they communicate... and the way they create wealth for themselves and their families.

The Right Place at the Right Time

Wouldn't you agree that timing is everything in business? The key to creating wealth is to get in at the right time... to get in a business explosion just before the boom... to catch the wave just as it starts to rise.

In the coming chapters, I'm going to share with you how you can catch two waves at the same time. The convergence of these two global megatrends will create a window of opportunity whereby average people can combine their natural-born talents as person-to-person networkers with the power of the Global Internet.

I call this opportunity your online dream business — Dream-Biz.com — because it combines all of the criteria for a dream business with the power and convenience of e-commerce. Best of all, it's a ground floor opportunity that's designed to take off like a rocket in the coming months and years.

Folks, there's no better time than the present to reserve your seat on the Dream-Biz.com rocket. And believe me, everyone on board will be in for the ride of a lifetime!

···8···

Network Marketing: A True "Dream Business"

I never think of my audience as customers. I think of them as partners.

–Jimmy Stewart, famous actor

We've all received letters from a mall announcing a "Grand Opening" or a "Huge Holiday Sale!" The wording of these letters may change from time to time, but the message is always the same: "GIVE US MORE OF YOUR HARD-EARNED MONEY."

Wouldn't it be great to receive a letter from a mall saying *they wanted to give you money*, instead of the other way around?

Here's the letter I'm *still* waiting to receive.

MEGA MALL
Suburb Avenue
Everywhere, USA

Dear Valued Customer:

Thank you again for using and recommending the products and services from the many stores in MegaMall.

Enclosed please find your monthly check, to include (1) rebates for the purchases you made personally; (2) your "advertising savings" bonus; and (3) your commissions on the purchases made by the friends, relatives, and acquaintances you referred to our mall.

MONTHLY STATEMENT

Rebate for personal purchases . . . . $ 20
Savings on monthly advertising . . . . $ 20
Commission on referral customers $400
Total $440

We appreciate your continuing support, and we look forward to sending you an even bigger check next month.

Sincerely,
Mr MegaMall Manager

How about you — have you ever received a letter like this from a place where you shop?

No?

I don't see why not.

You're a steady customer, aren't you? If you stopped shopping at the mall, they'd lose extra profits, wouldn't they?

Because of your recommendations, the mall doesn't need to advertise to you and your acquaintances anymore, so you deserve a refund on their ad savings, don't you?

And that referral fee is well earned, wouldn't you agree? After all, your person-to-person recommendation is the only reason your friends and acquaintances switched from a competitor's mall to buy at MegaMall, so your word-of-mouth marketing should be rewarded, isn't that true?

In fact, if it weren't for you, MegaMall revenues would be reduced by thousands of dollars, so it only makes sense that they reward you for bringing them business.

Fact, Not Fantasy

"Yeah, right!" you say to yourself. "When pigs fly! You're living in a Fantasy Land, Pal!"

Actually, this isn't fantasy — *this is fact.* Today many companies are offering discounts to loyal clients who bring in new business, plus the companies are encouraging their clients to partner with them by offering commissions and bonuses on the new business generated by their person-to-person referrals.

This concept of compensating people for recommending products and services they would use and recommend anyway goes by many names. It has been called referral marketing... person-to-person marketing... interactive distribution™... the alternative franchise™... and network marketing, to name a few.

I prefer to call the concept "network marketing" because we're all natural-born networkers, as we discussed earlier. It's natural for people to refer others to products and services they know their friends will enjoy. So why not compensate the person making the referral? That way everybody wins. It just makes sense.

How Network Marketing Works

Call it what you will, the business model of network marketing is easy to understand. A company makes or distributes a product or service. Then the company joins in partnership with a network of independent business owners. Here's how the partnership works:

The company takes care of all the big infrastructure expenses, such as manufacturing... packaging... quality control... warehousing... research and development... administration... employees... management... public relations... order processing... shipping... and payroll. In other words, all the headaches and major expenses.

About the only thing the company *doesn't* pay for that traditional businesses *do* pay for is advertising. And that's where the independent business owners come in. They market the products and services for the company. The company compensates independent business owners by paying them commissions and bonuses from the advertising money the company saves. How much might that calculate to be? Consider this. As much as 80% of a product's retail price can go for advertising.

Proctor and Gamble spends $2 billion every single year on advertising. Experts estimate that by the year 2000, companies will spend $200 billion a year advertising on TV, radio, newspapers, and the Internet (you didn't really think those little banners were free, did you?).

If that's not bad enough, companies aren't even sure if their expensive ads are working! Traditional advertising is like rolling the dice. As the famous advertising guru David Ogilvy put it, "Only 50% of every dollar spent on advertising works. Only problem is, we don't know which 50%."

A Win/Win Partnership

This partnership between the company and the independent business owner is a real win/win. The company gets the best form of advertising — word of mouth — from a legion of commission-only independent business owners. In addition, the company streamlines the distribution process. No more need for wholesalers... jobbers... brokers... salaried sales-persons... expensive retail outlets... store employ-ees and managers.

As a result, all of the middlemen and middle-women who would have had their fingers in the profit pie don't exist in the networking business model. The savings that result from this "lean and mean" operation can now be used to pay the inde-pendent business owners who are moving the prod-ucts, as the diagram below clearly illustrates:

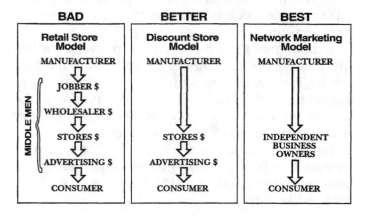

It's simple — brilliantly simple. *And it works like a charm!*

The independent business owners earn rebates and/or commissions on the products they use and sell, plus commissions on the sales generated by other business partners they bring into the business. Because there is no cap on their income or restric-tions on their territory, independent business own-ers have the incentive and the freedom to build huge organizations of consumers. It's not uncom-mon for an independent business owner to build an organization of consumers numbering in the 100s... or 1,000s... or 10,000s... or even more!

If each of those consumers averaged only $100 per month on products, and you built an organization of say, 1,000 consumers, you could earn commissions from 1% to 10%, or more, on $100,000 worth of product — each month!

How Network Marketing Grows

Now, you may be thinking, "Sounds interesting, but I could never build an organization of 1,000 consumers. I don't know that many people."

That's the best part of network marketing. Because of the power of a concept called "exponential growth," you don't have to personally talk to 1,000 people to earn commissions on the products they consume.

Exponential growth is what sets network marketing apart from franchising or any other business model, for that matter. In reality, even the most successful networkers only talk to a small fraction of the people in their organizations because they may number in the hundreds of thousands!

Remember the chart I used in Chapter 6 to explain how your personal internet might broadcast your message about a great movie you saw? It looked like this:

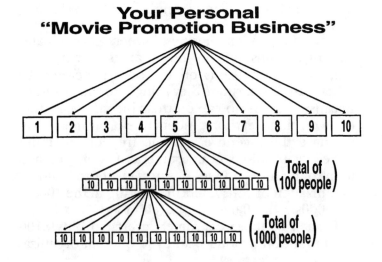

Your Personal "Movie Promotion Business"

Well, this time let's imagine that instead of telling people about a great movie, you told a bunch of people about a great business you just started. And let's assume only six of those people joined you in the business and duplicated your efforts, that is, they told a bunch of people and got six people to partner with them. Here's what the exponential growth chart for your networking business would look like:

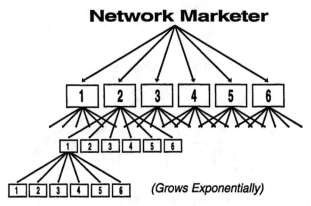

As you can plainly see, by partnering with six like-minded people in your new business and by teaching them to duplicate what you did throughout your organization, you'd be growing your business exponentially.

You see, exponential growth is what distinguishes network marketing from any other business model. Exponential growth means your business can potentially grow faster... and larger... than traditional businesses because they can only grow in a linear fashion.

Fuel-Injected Franchising

Networking is similar to another revolutionary business concept, franchising, in that each new "franchisee," also known as an independent business owner, duplicates and models a proven success formula. You can play the role of a franchisor by partnering with other people and teaching them a proven system for wealth creation.

But the similarities between networking and franchising end with duplication, for franchising can only grow in a staid *linear fashion*, as opposed to *exponential growth* of networking, which is dynamic. This is what the linear growth chart for your franchise-based system would look like:

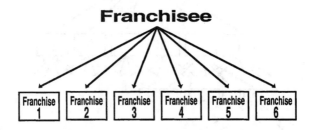

(Grows Linearly)

No matter how many additional franchises you acquire, the growth will always be linear. Which means you can never earn more than the total profits of your six franchises. In addition, networking companies don't restrict you to narrow territories, as franchisors do. If your parent company has a presence in a territory or country outside the U.S. and Canada, you can expand your business there, too.

Just One Person a Month Can Make You Rich

Do you think it would be possible to find just one person each month to join your business? Just one partner who's interested in more freedom, recognition, happiness, and security... one partner who's interested in improving the lives of his or her family?

One good person a month — that's all it takes!

Once you bring that person into the business with you, you become his or her business partner. Which means you don't need to concentrate all of your efforts on selling the products. You need to teach, coach, and help other people.

Now, going into month two, there are two of you working together. You help your new partner find a partner, while you bring on another partner. So, at the end of month two, you've personally brought in two new independent business owners and your first partner has brought in a partner as well. Now you have a group of four — you and three others.

You do the same for month three... four... five... and so on. At the end of your first year, you will have personally brought in 12 new partners, one each month. And let's assume each of those has brought in one new partner as well... and so on, down the line.

Now you'll see the awesome power of exponential growth at work. At the end of the year, just by bringing in one new person a month and teaching each of those people to do the same — *you could have an organization of 4,096 people!*

Now do you see why I say network marketing is like fuel-injected franchising? It uses the power of duplication just like franchising, but it supercharges the growth by way of the exponential factor.

Networking: A True Dream Business

You might say that *network marketing takes the best of the franchising concept...* but leaves the rest! It capitalizes on the power of exponential growth, but it's much more affordable than franchising... AND it can grow like wildfire!

That's why I call network marketing a "dream business." Let's review the criteria for a dream business and then briefly discuss how network marketing meets each one of the criterion.

How Network Marketing Meets
the Five Criteria for a Dream Business

1) *Residual income:* Residual income is when you do the work once and you keep getting paid over and over. Networking certainly qualifies on this one. Some networkers have been earning money from people they introduced to the business 25 years ago or more. That's residual!

2) *Global market:* If your network marketing company has a presence in a country or territory, you can, too. Some companies are in as many as 80 countries and territories.

3) *Willable and sellable:* One networking company has third-generation people working the business and all the original lines of sponsorship are still being honored. Is that willable enough for you? Your organization is sellable, too. But who would want to sell a dream business anyway?

4) *Duplicatable:* The support system of books, tapes, and live events is there to help you succeed. Tie into the system, and then duplicate yourself by teaching others to do the same.

5) *Low investment & low maintenance:* This may be the best feature of the business. The cost of entry is so low that it's available to virtually anyone. The opportunity is open to all comers. As far as low maintenance, most networkers prefer to work out of their homes, even the hugely successful networkers who can afford to *buy* a high-rise office building. It's not *where* you work but *how* you work that counts in this business.

There you have it — a dream business that grows exponentially. What more could you ask for? Now you understand the power of network marketing and why it's truly a dream business.

Now it's time to talk a little history.

Network Marketing Is 100 Years Young

In 1892, Richard Sears, founder of Sears, Roebuck and Co., opened a catalog business. Sears was a marketing innovator to beat all innovators, and he was determined to grow the biggest catalog company in the country.

To increase the circulation of his catalogs, Sears gave his best customers 24 free catalogs to distribute to their friends and relatives. In return, when the recipients placed an order, Sears awarded their "sponsors" points toward free merchandise! Pretty clever, eh?

As a result of Richard Sears' innovative marketing, his business grew so fast that within eight years, he surpassed Montgomery Ward, a company that had a 20-year head start, as the largest mail order catalog in the U.S. Word-of-mouth, person-to-person marketing helped launch Sears, Roebuck and Co. into one of the world's greatest companies.

Fast forward to 1940. A company called California Vitamins discovered that all of their sales reps started out as satisfied customers. The company also discovered it was a lot easier to get a whole lot of people to use and sell a little product than it was to find a few superstars who could sell a whole bunch by themselves.

So, the company combined those two ideas and designed a marketing and compensation structure that encouraged their sales people to recruit new distribution partners from the ranks of satisfied customers, most of whom were family and friends. The company rewarded the sales staff by giving them a percentage of the sales produced by their entire group.

The results were staggering! Even though each individual in a distribution network only sold a couple hundred dollars' worth of products each month, all of the groups combined moved tens of thousands of dollars' worth of vitamins!

Network marketing was born.

A few years later, the company changed its name to Nutrilite. Two of its most successful distributors were Jay Van Andel and Rich DeVos. They went on to start their own network marketing company — Amway. Today, these two gentlemen are multi-billionaires. And to think they started out as independent business owners in network marketing!

Where Network Marketing Is Today

Today network marketing is going global, sweeping North America and the world. There are thousands of networking companies operating in nearly 100 countries. Malaysia alone has more than 800 active network marketing companies.

Network marketing is reported to be a $100 billion international industry, made up of Fortune 500 and New York Stock Exchange (NYSE) companies, including Avon — the $3 billion cosmetic giant. Amway, marching toward $10 billion in world-wide sales. Primerica — the Dow Jones insurance and financial services multi-national. And the list of household names goes on — Shaklee, Tupperware, Rexall, Mary Kay Cosmetics.

Colgate-Palmolive and The Gillette Company have network marketing subsidiaries. In recent years, US Sprint and MCI generated more than three million new customers by networking their long-distance services. And a sizable number of those customers were taken from giant AT&T. So how did AT&T fight back? By contracting with several networking companies to help distribute their services! Hey, you don't get to be a billion-dollar company by being dumb!

Network Marketing and Technology

Network marketing didn't get to where it was during Richard Sears' day to where it is today without making major adjustments along the way. Just as Sears department stores changed with the times by doing away with what used to be the backbone of their business — their catalog — network marketing has survived by adapting to change.

In fact, network marketing has always been on the leading edge of change... out in front of the pack, embracing breakthrough technological tools as they entered the market.

Independent business owners with networking companies were among the first users of audio and numeric pagers... fax machines... cellular phones... tele-conferencing... video conferencing... video and audio training tapes... voice mail... personal computers... satellite broadcasts... e-mail... and on and on. You name the technology, and you'll discover that networkers were among the first to buy it, use it, and leverage it to help them move their products and build their businesses.

Welcoming Technology with Open Arms

Unlike many traditional businesses that resist change, network marketing invites change. The entrepreneurial environment encourages innovation and rewards efficiency. If you can show network marketers how to move more product more quickly and how to build stronger relationships, they're all ears.

Whenever the latest technology hits the marketplace, networkers ask two questions: One, will it help me leverage my time, reach more people, and build better relationships? And two, is it affordable and duplicatable? If the answer is "yes" to those questions, then the next obvious question is, "Where can I get it, and when can I get started?"

Just compare the positive, proactive attitude of a networker to the negative, reactive attitude of most employees in traditional businesses: *"I've done it this way for seven years, and I've only got three more years before retirement. Why do I need to use e-mail? They wanna talk to me, Honey? They can call me!"*

Responding to the Internet

Right now the network marketing industry is positioning itself to exploit the greatest technological tool ever invented — the PC with Internet access. Networking companies and their independent business owners have been appraising the Internet for some time now... sizing up its potential... thinking about possible applications... asking the key questions:

"Can the Internet help me leverage my time, reach more people, and build better relationships? And is it affordable and duplicatable?"

The industry wasn't sure of the answers to these questions, as the Internet was changing so rapidly that it was hard for even the brightest, most innovative business people to get a fix on this amazing technology.

Don't forget, Bill Gates passed on the Internet when he first saw it. He thought it was much ado about nothing — an amazing technology, but no real purpose. But when Gates took a second look a few months later, his vision cleared, and he suddenly recognized the Net's enormous potential.

Within months of Gates' revelation, Microsoft became a dominant Internet player — developing the Internet Explorer browser... forging online alliances... buying Internet companies... investing in cable TV companies... arranging dozens of creative joint ventures.

Today Microsoft is totally committed to the Internet, and the company is re-engineering itself, changing its focus from software production to Internet applications.

Time for a Talk with "Junior"

The network marketing industry is following Gates' lead. No more hesitation. No more, "Let's-wait-and-see." The forward-looking networking companies are re-engineering themselves, partnering with Internet experts to adapt the networking business model to the Internet.

It's obvious why network marketing companies would be interested in the Internet. E-commerce is booming. The technology is fast... vast... affordable... convenient... and growing at an astronomical rate. Networking needs the Internet, just as it has needed cell phones and fax machines.

Is that to say that network marketing cannot survive without e-commerce?

Silly question — of course it can!

Network marketing has been a thriving, growing industry for more than 50 years, long before mainframe computers were even built. But computers and all of the other technological advancements sure made it a lot easier for networking companies and their independent business owners to grow their businesses.

Same goes for the technology of the Internet. Network marketing can choose to live without the Internet... or networkers can choose to use Internet technology to help them grow to the next level, just as they did with fax machines and cellular phones.

Now let's reverse the question: What does network marketing offer the Internet? What does networking bring to the banquet? At first glance, it may look as if networking doesn't have much to offer the "new kid on the block." Looks like the Internet has the world on a string, and the string around its finger.

"What ya' got for me, Mr. Network Marketing Company?" says the Internet. "Looks like I don't need you. You need me!"

The Internet crosses his cyberarms, puffs out his chest, and smiles confidently.

Network Marketing doesn't even blink.

"*Sit down, Kid,*" says Network Marketing. "*I think it's time you and I had a little talk.*"

Part Three

e-Networking: The Marriage of e-Commerce and Network Marketing

...9...

Why e-Commerce Needs Network Marketing — Now!

> *It is not enough to wire the world if you short-circuit the soul. Technology without heart is not enough.*
>
> –Tom Brokaw, NBC News Anchor

[Let's listen in on an historical conversation between Network Marketing and the Internet — a conversation that is destined to revolutionize the economy in the New Millennium.]

Network Marketing decided it was time to sit down with the young, ambitious Internet for a little heart-to-heart talk. Network Marketing liked this Kid called The Internet. The Kid kind of reminded networking of himself when he was younger. Brash. Bold. Daring. Refusing to play by the rules — in fact, making up the rules as he went along.

The Kid has a lot of raw talent, no doubt about that. But he's getting pretty arrogant and cocky. So it was time for a talk. Network Marketing didn't want to break the Kid's spirit — just wanted to give him direction. With a little mentoring, this Kid could really be something.

"What was that you said earlier?" asked Network Marketing in mock seriousness. *"Something about how 'I need you, but that you don't necessarily need me?'"* The old veteran Network Marketing was baiting the Internet. He knew the Kid was too full of himself to notice.

"I believe my precise words were, 'Looks like I don't need you. You need me,' replied the Internet. "I'm digitized, you know. So I have a photographic memory. Unlike you, I don't make mistakes. You, on the other hand, are nothing but a mass of people. Which means you're prone to human error. You're emotional. Individualistic. Hard to control. You dislike change, and you're a slow learner.

"Yeah, Mr. Networker. I'd say you need me, all right. I'm just not sure you're what I'm looking for. You and I both know I have the world at my terminal! In fact, I can't think of one good reason I should even consider partnering with you!"

Network Marketing listened patiently. The Kid was full of himself, no doubt about that. He was on the cutting edge of technology and he knew it! But over the years Network Marketing learned to be wise.

He'd learned the importance of understanding the person you were talking with. He knew you could turn off prospects if you took the wrong approach. He'd learned from experience to read between the lines. And what the Networker read was that the Kid was desperate for the right partner. This was the only opening the Networker needed.

"Who said anything about partnering?" Network Marketing asked nonchalantly.

The Kid's cocky expression morphed into a frown. He had spilled the beans and he knew it.

"Did I use the word 'partnering'?" the Kid asked innocently.

"You're the one with the digitized memory," the Networker said casually. *"Play it back. I believe your exact words were, 'I can't think of one good reason I should even consider partnering with you!' But then, my memory isn't as good as yours, is it?"*

The Internet realized immediately that he'd made a strategic blunder. Now the Network Marketer had the advantage. The Internet's server whirred and clicked, calculating in seconds the millions of options. He decided to remain silent and wait for the Networker to reply.

The Networker used the long, awkward silence to plan his approach. He knew the Kid was rational. Logical to a fault. Give him the facts. He needed to deliver his message without emotion. Data wins the day with this guy. Lay out the features and benefits in short, simple statements. This is it — the moment of truth. No more beating around the bush. Get to a yes or no. Maybes will kill you.

"Okay, Kid," said the Network Marketer, squaring his shoulders. *No more games. From here forward we deal in data — the cold, hard facts. You like what you hear, we shake hands, and we walk out of here as partners. You don't like the deal, we walk away from the table. No hard feelings. Like I always say, 'I'm going to do this business with or without you.' I'd like to do it with you. And here are the reasons why.*

"First of all, I want to tell you that I think you're the greatest technology to come along since the invention of the automobile. You've come a long way in a short time. You've got great work habits, online 24 hours a day. You help the world send and receive information at the speed of light. You've put

up some impressive numbers. But let's face it — you're strug-
gling. You're getting lots of visitors to your sites, but most of
them are just hits, not buys. Right now your customers have
no loyalty to you."

The Networker paused to make sure his message
entered the Internet's data banks. He didn't want
his message to float around in cyberspace. He wanted this e-mail delivered right now!

"We both know lack of loyalty is taking its toll on you,"
Network Marketing continued. "You have to spend billions of
dollars in advertising to lure customers to your websites, and
you never know if they'll even buy anything, much less if
they'll become regular customers. Let's face it — your customers have no allegiance to you because they aren't emotion-
ally involved with you, like a good friend would be. Your customers come and go like the wind, and you have to spend a
big part of your profits attracting new people. What you need
is repeat business. This is where I come in."

The Networker chose to open with his strongest
arguments first. This was no time to tip-toe through
the issues. Get right to the crux of the issue and
then build momentum from there.

"Look, you and I both know that the one thing you need
are people who buy your products or services month in and
month out. You need clients who are loyal to your brands...
loyal to the company... and loyal to the relationship.

"What do you think would happen if you started treating
your customers as clients and partners, like we do? You'd see
your bottom line start to soar like the space shuttle heading
into orbit, isn't that true?"

The Networker knew he'd hit the Kid right
between the eyes. He knew he'd gotten the
Internet's attention with the loyalty argument and
by bringing up the Internet's Achilles' heel — the
fact that lots of e-commerce companies are making
big revenues, but only a few are showing a profit. E-
commerce needed a solution — and fast! Network
Marketing decided to launch right into the reason
that so many e-commerce sites were losing money

despite posting huge gross revenues.

"You're spending a small fortune on advertising trying to attract new customers," the Networker continued. "And as soon as you get one, they run over to your competitor because he's offering it for a nickel less. We Network Marketers, on the other hand, use the most effective advertising known to humans — relationship marketing. Person-to-person, word-of-mouth marketing. A thousand banner ads can't equal the value of one sincere person referring a product or service to a friend. You and I both know that.

"We appreciate and practice loyalty," the Networker continued. "We build our businesses by building relationships first. We have automatic standing orders for our products. We offer one-of-a-kind, brand-name products that need to be replenished monthly. And we have brand loyalty, something you desperately need. We don't believe that throwing your money away on banner ads is an effective way to build a large, PROFITABLE business that will be around 20 years from now."

The Networker leaned on the word "profitable," because he knew it went straight to the heart of the matter. Despite the enormous potential of e-commerce, only a handful of the thousands of e-commerce sites were profitable. Their day of reckoning was getting close at hand, and they knew it.

"The people in our industry have a bond. They think and work like a community. They cheer for each other. They inspire each other. They form life-long relationships. They attend positive, uplifting meetings and events where they learn to sharpen their skills and improve their attitudes. And yes, they even attend church together. Our people think and act as a team.

"But what about your people?" the Networker continued. "Do they share a common vision or goal? Do they have a sense of community or shared purpose? Do they strive to help each other in times of need? Or are your people splintered? Untrained? And unfocused? What do you think would happen in a time of crisis? Would they pull together as one — or would they pull out and jump ship to the next deal?"

The Networker knew that the Internet was no dummy. The message was getting through, loud and clear.

"Here's the bottom line, Kid. You need what we have, and you know it. We can bring you the power of group purchasing, loyal customers, predictable monthly consumers, and lots of traffic without advertising. We've got 50 years of experience to your five, and we're experts in manufacturing and distribution, something you're still trying to get the hang of. I can direct as many as a million eyeballs to one website in a matter of days, and I'm not talking 'hits' — I'm talking loyal product users.

"Once my independent business owners start directing e-commerce traffic," Network Marketing continued, *"there's no telling how much product you can move through one of your sites. You're so desperate for customers that you're trying to low-ball every product. First lesson in commerce, Kid. The lowest price isn't necessarily the best value. First thing we'll do when we partner is teach you how to build value through trusting relationships. And that, Kid, is why you need me more than I need you."*

The Networker locked eyes with the Internet and leaned forward in his chair. He decided to let the words sink in. He knew the Internet had processed the information. The Kid was fast. Real fast. But there was more at stake here than some simple calculations. What was at stake was the future of distribution. This was an historic moment. This was the moment of truth, and both of them knew it.

The Networker studied the Kid. He had talent and brains, all right. But he lacked the human leadership it takes to make it big in the e-economy. The Networker knew he had to take the lead.

So he slowly extended his hand across the table.

"Together we can make history, Kid. Let's partner up and make the world a better place to live and work. Millions of people with unfulfilled dreams need us working together as a team."

The Networker's arm hung in the air, his hand strong and steady. The Kid remained expressionless. The Networker's gaze remained fixed, unblinking, on the Internet's face. The Kid met his gaze straight on.

"What do you say — are we partners?" the Networker asked sincerely.

The Networker felt a firm hand meet his. The movement was fast... the speed of light. The Networker looked down at the firm handshake, and then back to the Internet's face, which revealed bright eyes and a wide smile.

"Hello, partner," said the Internet.

"Hello, partner," replied the Network Marketer.

··· 10 ···

e-Networking: The Marriage of e-Commerce and Network Marketing

Smart companies will combine Internet services and personal contact in programs that give their customers the benefits of both kinds of interaction.

—Bill Gates, from *Business @ the Speed of Light*

Think outside the box.

What a great concept — to think OUTSIDE the box!

When we think outside the box, it frees us to become much more creative in our approach to solving problems. Instead of accepting WHAT IS, we start thinking about WHAT COULD BE. The result is often a new and better way of working and/or living.

The marriage of e-commerce and network marketing is a perfect example of thinking outside the box. E-commerce is the business of the future. Network marketing is a dream business. If they're doing great separately, just think what they could do together.

Think outside the box!

Let's see... if you married e-commerce with network marketing, what would you get? Let's do the math:

e-commerce + network marketing = e-networking

That's it — *e-networking!* It only makes sense!

You take a revolutionary business model with a 50-year history — *network marketing*. And you marry it with a revolutionary business model of the New Millennium — *e-commerce*. And what do you get? You'd get e-networking, a marriage made in heaven! You'd get the electronic part of e-commerce plus the people-part of networking. Together they would make e-networking, an e-commerce business that grows exponentially. It's the next economic revolution! *It's a no-brainer!*

With e-networking, you'd have all of the advantages of a dream business plus all of the advantages of an e-commerce business. You'd have a dream business at the speed of light. You'd have a new business model based on e-networking — in other words, a *Dream-Biz.com!*

What If...?

Think outside the box!

What would your Dream-Biz.com look like? Let's do some possibility thinking!

What if a network marketing company set up a "digital destination" that included a virtual mall and made their products plus other name-brand products available over the Internet?

What if the independent business owners could sign up people electronically instead of on paper?

What if the company used e-mail and its website to communicate with the distributors and product users?

What if the website educated people about the products and answered their questions for them?

What if the "digital destination" included a virtual office (along with the virtual mall) so that independent business owners could share their opportunity with others?

What if visitors to the website could buy products at retail?... or, for a small annual fee, could become a member of a Dream-Biz.com buyers' club and receive discounts and credit for referring their friends and neighbors to the site?

What if independent business owners could build their business by directing people to the virtual mall and earn commissions on any of the products purchased by their new clients or business partners... plus earn commissions on the products purchased by THEIR clients and partners, and so on down the line?

What if the networking company took the best features of e-commerce — its speed, efficiency, and global reach — and added the best part of network marketing — its person-to-person marketing of products and its sharing and caring method of building a business?

What if an established networking company did all that — AND MORE? Would that be thinking out of the box? Would that be a Dream-Biz.com? Would that be possible?

It's Possible... and It's Happening

It's not only possible — it's about to become a reality. According to a cover story in *USA Today*, a new company called Quixtar (pronounced "quick-star") will be open for business on the Internet September 1, 1999. According to the article, marketing consultant Ken Harris of Cannondale Associates says, "I believe Quixtar will be a $3 billion to $5 billion business in its first year."

"The personal contact is pretty powerful," Harris goes on to say. He's not alone in his rosy assessment of Quixtar. The article quotes David Rush, a retail consultant with Kurt Salmon Associates as saying, "Externally, I see nothing but wins here."

According to an article in the business section of *Newsday*, Quixtar is being moved online by two powerful high-tech partners, Microsoft and IBM. The article describes Quixtar as "the name of a company, a Web site and a business plan," which pretty well sums up this radical enterprise.

The people behind this e-networking venture are none other than the founders of The Amway Corporation, the granddaddy of granddaddies when it comes to network marketing. The DeVos and Van Andel families are the driving force behind this radical new business model named Quixtar. The combination of the founders' vast entrepreneurial experience, coupled with the multi-billion dollar resources of the Amway Corporation, bodes well for the future of e-networking.

I'm a Champion of the Industry

Let me make one thing perfectly clear. As I mentioned in my first book, *Who Stole the American Dream?*, I'm not a distributor for any network marketing company. I'm impartial... third party... and unbiased. I just tell it like I see it. My first, last, and only commitment is to the legitimate companies and the honest, hard-working distributors in the industry.

Here's the original statement I made about Amway in *Who Stole the American Dream?*, and this statement applies today just as much as it did when I first wrote it back in 1991.

> *"I believe in giving credit where credit is due, and I believe the network marketing industry owes Amway a big debt of gratitude. They were the first major players in a revolutionary experiment... they were the Model T Ford version of a brave new industry. It's because of them that major companies are now involved (and more are becoming involved every day) in network marketing."*

I see history repeating itself here. Once again the founders of Amway are major players in a revolutionary business model. This one is called Quixtar. I believe Quixtar will pioneer the way for e-networking. As I said, let's give credit where credit is due.

Radical Business Model for a Radical New Millennium

As radical as this business model may sound, there have been many paradigm-shattering products born from thinking out of the box.

You marry a horse-drawn carriage with the internal combustion engine, and what do you get? A revolutionary product — *the automobile!*

You marry a typewriter with a calculator, and what do you get? A revolutionary product — *the personal computer!*

You marry a phone with a copier, and what do you get? A revolutionary product — *the fax machine!*

You marry e-commerce with network marketing, and what do you get? A revolutionary product — *e-networking!* You get a revolutionary business model whereby average people can grow their e-commerce business exponentially. It's revolutionary. It's out of the box. And it's a no-brainer.

This thing only makes sense. I know it's a revolutionary business model. But the automobile was revolutionary for its time, too. So was the personal computer. And so was the fax machine. Can you imagine a world without these products? All of them are marvelous tools that changed the way people live and work.

So, get radical!

Open your mind.

Think out of the box.

Think e-networking.

Think Dream-Biz.com.

··· 11 ···

The More High Tech We Have, the More High Touch We Need!

The more technology we introduce into society, the more people will want to aggregate, will want to be with other people.

—John Naisbitt, from *Megatrends*

It's hard to believe that John Naisbitt's modern classic, *Megatrends*, is nearing 20 years old. I'm delighted to report that the book has passed the test of time with flying colors!

First published in 1982, *Megatrends* discusses the 10 key trends that will transform our lives well into the 21st century. Amazingly, all of his forecasts were right on the money — especially his observation that the more the world becomes high tech, the more we need high touch.

High Tech/High Touch

"Whenever new technology is introduced into society, there must be a counterbalancing human response — that is, *high touch...*," says Naisbitt. Examples of this phenomenon are all around us.

Naisbitt cites the hospice movement as the human, "high touch" response to the cold, "high tech" life support systems routinely used in hospitals today. Another example is the human potential movement. Naisbitt contends that the vast majority of people interested in personal growth are the baby boomers, who were bombarded by TV when they were growing up. They're balancing their high tech childhood experience with high touch personal growth books, tapes, and seminars.

Balancing the Hard Edges of e-Commerce

Naisbitt understood that humans have an inborn need to balance the hard machine edges of high tech with the soft human edges of high touch. And that need for balance applies to the high tech Internet just as much as it applies to high tech medical equipment.

Can you guess what customers at e-commerce sites request most often? If you guessed cheaper products or faster delivery, you'd be wrong. According to a random survey of e-commerce shoppers, *what online shoppers most requested was a live person to talk to!* High tech/high touch.

Enter network marketing.

Network marketing is the high touch counterbalance that e-commerce needs to offset its high tech edge. You see, successful networkers understand that they're in the people business — first, last, and foremost. Products don't order products — *people order products!* Products can't direct traffic to a website — *people direct traffic!* Cell phones, fax machines, and e-commerce don't grow a networker's business — *people grow their businesses!* Networking has always been a high touch people business, and more than anything else, e-commerce needs high touch people!

In Naisbitt's words, "Whenever institutions introduce new technology to customers or employees, they should build in a high touch component." That's why e-networking is such a natural — it combines the greatest high tech tool ever invented — the Internet... with the greatest high touch business ever invented — network marketing. I'm telling you, it's a marriage made in heaven!

You Gotta Have Heart

I get the feeling some veteran networkers are fearful that e-commerce will take over their business and push them to the side. *That will never happen!* E-commerce needs the high touch component that networking offers.

There's no substitute for a warm heart. None! Everyone needs to be around people who care. We need recognition from others for a job well done. We need a soft shoulder to cry on when we're hurting. We need a spirited, joyful person to celebrate with when we reach our goals.

Only people can give other people the "tions" that we all need. "What are the *tions?*" you ask. The "tions" are the things we crave and need the most in this world.

Atten-*tion.*
Inspira-*tion.*
Motiva-*tion.*
Celebra-*tion.*
Recogni-*tion.*

Valida-*tion.*
Dedica-*tion.*

Those are just a few of the "tions." They'll never invent a "tion" machine. All a high tech machine can do is help facilitate the high touch connection between people. A phone call from the right person at the right time, for example, has helped mend many a broken heart. What people are really after isn't the phone call — it's the voice of a human on the other end cheering them on:

"You can do it!"
"Don't quit!"
"I know how you feel, I felt the same way!"
"You've got to be strong!"
"Keep your eyes on the prize!"
"I'm SO proud of you!"
"You're the best!"
"I love you!"

High touch is the human touch, and there's nothing else quite like it!

Values-Driven

There's another high touch component people need that the Internet can't address. I'm talking about positive values — the values that made this nation strong... the values we try to pass along to our children.

As we're all aware, the Internet is a wide-open medium. It's like a visit to New York City. There are a lot of great things to see there — wonderful stores and world-class museums and spectacular Broadway musicals. But there are a lot of places you're better off avoiding in the Big Apple. Take a wrong turn or hook up with the wrong person, and you may live to regret it.

Same with the Internet. There's a lot of great stuff happening on the Internet. But there are a lot of bad things you need to avoid... a lot of websites that you don't want your children visiting... a lot of scams aimed at naive users. Take a wrong turn on the Internet or hook up with the wrong website, and you may live to regret it.

The Internet is only a tool. As such, it's an amoral machine. It doesn't know whether it's passing along inspiration from Scripture or a deadly computer virus — and it doesn't care.

That's where high touch comes in. If you limit your visits to sites you can trust or to Internet malls that are backed by reputable companies with a history of values-driven leadership, you'll be in good shape.

Person-to-Person Training

One final thought on high tech/high touch and the Internet. The people who are building the Internet and who develop the websites for e-commerce are real computer nerds. "Total techies," I call them. Sometimes they're so smart they can't understand just how non-technical the average person really is.

Only a small minority of the population can be classified as total techies. The vast majority of people don't know the first thing about computers. Because they've had bad experiences with technical gadgets in the past, they have a lot of anxieties and fears about getting hooked up on the Internet.

They don't know which computer to buy. They wouldn't know the first thing about setting up a brand new PC... much less which Internet service provider they should use or how to surf the Net and use e-mail. They're not dumb. They just need some high touch help and reassurance, and they need a person to answer their questions when they get started.

Enter network marketing again. Networkers have a long history of teaching and coaching others. When an independent business owner brings you in as a partner, you can bet he or she will help you get up and running on the Internet in no time. Then once you get comfortable surfing the Net, you'll help your new partners do the same.

E-networking — it's a win/win. It's high tech/high touch. It's a virtual mall/virtual business. Are you beginning to see how a dream business that grows exponentially can evolve into a Dream-Biz.com through the power of e-commerce?

This is a once-in-a-lifetime opportunity, folks. *And it's only a point and a click away!*

...12...

Timing Is Everything in Life and Business!

The Internet will become as fundamental tomorrow as the automobile is today.
—Bill Gates

The year is 1903. Henry Ford, a trusted friend of yours, asks you to invest $1,000 in his new business, Ford Motor Company. You have the wisdom to lend Ford the money.

What do you think a $1,000 investment in Ford Motor Company back in 1903 would be worth just 15 years later? A million? Ten million? *How about $35 million!*

What follows is a true story of one lucky investor... and it proves that timing is everything in life and business. Henry Ford raised $28,000 from nine investors to start his company. One investor contributed $1,000 cash plus $1,500 in assets that Ford could borrow against if he needed it.

In 1919, just 15 years later, Ford decided to buy out his original investors. Up to this point, the $1,000 cash investment had returned $5 million in dividends to that one lucky investor. Pretty good return, wouldn't you say?

But wait — that was only the beginning. *Ford wrote the lucky investor a check for $30 million to buy out all of his remaining shares.*

Recognizing a Window of Opportunity

At first glance it looks like Henry Ford got the short end of the stick. But Ford knew $30 million was a drop in the bucket compared to what the company would earn in the years ahead. You see, he recognized that the window of opportunity had been flung wide open. Cars sales were poised to explode!

Henry Ford knew that the big money hadn't been made yet — and he was right. Automobiles went from 10% market penetration in 1915 to 90% during the next 15 years. Which means that the year Ford bought all of his stock back, his company was just entering the boom years! The graph on the top of the next page clearly shows that the window of opportunity had opened wide to the automobile industry in 1918.

WINDOW OF OPPORTUNITY
at the Turn of 20th Century

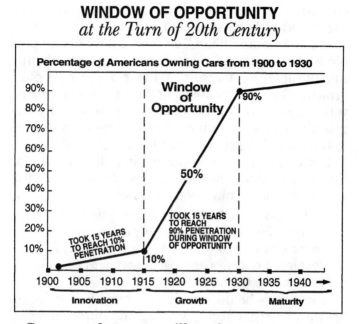

Percentage of Americans Owning Cars from 1900 to 1930

Car manufacturers still make money, as evidenced by GM, which has led the world in gross revenues 11 years running. But the opportunity for fast, dynamic growth has been over for decades. The once wide-open window of opportunity is open just a crack now. Today a $1,000 investment in Ford Motor Company might return 10% a year, if you're lucky. The boom years are over.

The Roaring 2000s

The graph above is based on data from the bestselling book, *The Roaring 2000s*. The author, Harry S. Dent, Jr., says we're just now entering the greatest economic boom in world history, largely due to the fact that the baby boom generation is entering its peak spending years. Dent calls this period, "the roaring 2000s," an obvious parallel to the roaring '20s when Henry Ford made his enormous fortune.

Led by the baby boomer generation — which is four times the size of the previous generation —

consumers will spend trillions of dollars in the coming decade. Who stands to benefit the most from "the great boom ahead," as Dent calls it? The people who recognize the windows of opportunity that will fly open as a result of the massive economic growth. The key to building your future and living your dreams in the e-economy is to identify the growth products and industries — and then to position yourself to profit from the new growth.

Dent singles out computers and the Internet as the twin engines that will power the astronomical growth in the coming boom years:

> *"The Internet is to the coming economic boom, the Roaring 2000s, what the moving assembly line was to the Roaring '20s. It is the key productivity lever that will rapidly feed new technologies, products, and services into the mainstream economy."*

The graph below clearly illustrates how computers with Internet access will explode during the first decade of the 21st century:

WINDOW OF OPPORTUNITY
@ the Turn of 21st Century

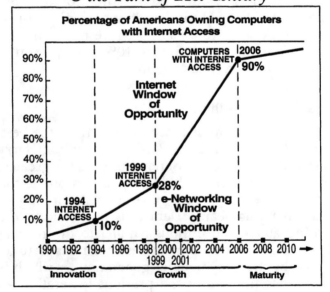

As this graph shows, only 10% of the population was online in 1994. As I write this in 1999, 28% of homes are online and traffic is doubling every 100 days. Forrester Research predicts 50% of U.S. households will be online by 2003.

Computer sales and Internet traffic will spur growth in each other. Dent predicts that by 2006, 90% of the households in North America will own PCs. As the popularity of the Internet increases and prices for online services come down, it's a cinch that Internet use will grow right along with PCs.

In Dent's words, "The Internet represents the accelerator, the consumer-oriented innovation that will propel the network revolution into the mainstream over the coming decade."

A Wise Man Investigates

Let's review the facts one more time.

- Almost 25% of the American population — the baby boomers — are now entering their peak spending years.

- Today 28% of the homes have Internet access, and it's predicted that 90% will be online by 2006.

- Each day 15,000 new subscribers log onto the Internet; traffic doubles every 100 days.

- Conservative estimates predict e-commerce will grow more than 20-fold from $4.5 billion in 1998... to $115 billion in 2005 (although some experts predict e-commerce could easily reach $1 trillion by 2005).

What do all of these megatrends mean for e-commerce? They mean e-commerce is going to continue to explode well into the 21st century! It's a done deal. It's happening, and it's just going to get *bigger and bigger and bigger!*

People are going to make vast fortunes during the coming boom. Do you want to sit this one out? Or do you want to claim your share of this global-size economic pie? Folks, this thing is so big there's room enough for all of us. There has never been a better time than the present to position yourself to profit from the e-commerce explosion.

You don't need to be a genius industrialist, like Henry Ford, to profit from this boom. You just need to be like the lucky investor, an average guy who happened to be in the right place at the right time. You need to *recognize your opportunity... and then take action!*

Opportunity of the New Millennium

E-networking is an opportunity whose time has come. Through e-networking, you can build an e-commerce business exponentially! Folks, this is a no brainer! A slam dunk! Thousands of people all over the world are going to make a fortune on this opportunity — you might as well be one of them!

Two revolutionary business models — network marketing and e-commerce — have converged to create your Dream-Biz.com, the opportunity of the millennium!

You don't have to become a statistic in the income gap... or settle for the dream gap!

You're finally in the right place at the right time! *The window of opportunity is wide open!*

Folks, don't let regrets take the place of your dreams — instead, believe in the beauty of your dreams!

I challenge you to take advantage of an opportunity whose time has come.

I challenge you to *design your future... and live your dreams!*